THE HOMEOWNER'S GUIDE TO SELLING

A COMPLETE FSBO HANDBOOK
FOR MAXIMUM PROFIT

GREGORY REICHMUTH

ISBN: 978-1-965957-30-1 Digital
ISBN: 978-1-965957-31-8 EPUB
ISBN: 978-1-965957-32-5 Paperback
ISBN: 978-1-965957-33-2 Hardcover

DIY Flex Realty
Email: Gregory@DIYFlexrealty.com
Website:www.DIYFlexRealty.com

This book is intended for informational purposes only. The author and publisher make no representations or warranties regarding the completeness or accuracy of the contents, and the reader assumes all responsibility for actions taken based on this information. Readers are advised to consult legal or financial professionals for specific guidance related to their unique circumstances.

First Edition

Printed in the United States of America

Dedication

To my beloved mother, Barbara Ann Reichmuth (1941 - 2024).

Your unwavering love, wisdom, and inspiration have shaped the person I am today. Your strength, kindness, and dedication to our family and your endless encouragement to pursue my dreams will forever be remembered and cherished.

This book series is dedicated to you, Mom. Your spirit lives on in every word, and your legacy of inspiration continues to guide me. Thank you for being my guiding light and my greatest supporter. I love you and miss you every day.

In loving memory,
Gregory Reichmuth

Legal Disclosure

The information contained in this book, The Homeowner's Guide to Selling: A Complete FSBO Handbook for Maximum Profit, is provided for general informational and educational purposes only. It is not intended to constitute legal, financial, or real estate advice, nor does it establish a professional-client relationship between the author and the reader.

While every effort has been made to ensure the accuracy and completeness of the information presented, real estate laws, market conditions, and practices may vary by location and are subject to change over time. Readers are encouraged to consult with licensed professionals, including attorneys, real estate agents, accountants, or other qualified experts, to address their specific circumstances before making any decisions or undertaking any real estate transactions.

FOREWORD

Gregory Reichmuth

Brings over 30 years of hands-on experience in real estate marketing, encompassing everything from fix-and-flip investments to managing rental properties. As a licensed real estate broker in Colorado since 2019, Gregory has built a career based on a deep understanding of both the traditional and innovative aspects of real estate sales. His experiences have shaped a unique perspective on the For Sale By Owner (FSBO) process, which is the heart of this guide.

Through his work at **DIY Flex Realty**, an independently operated real estate company, Gregory has championed a mission to make real estate transactions accessible, affordable, and empowering for homeowners. DIY Flex Realty is committed to a transparent, flat-fee service model that allows sellers to access only the services they truly need. Unlike traditional brokerage structures, DIY Flex Realty provides **scaled services** for sellers, tailored to fit the unique demands of FSBO transactions.

Whether it's listing guidance, marketing support, or document preparation, DIY Flex Realty gives homeowners the freedom to choose how much support they want in their sale journey. The goal is to offer sellers a practical, budget-friendly alternative to high commission rates, without compromising on quality or professionalism. This approach aligns seamlessly with the spirit of FSBO, where control, flexibility, and cost-savings are paramount.

With this book, Gregory aims to pass on the insights and strategies that have proven effective in countless FSBO transactions. Here, you'll find actionable guidance designed for both first-time sellers and seasoned homeowners who want to maintain full control over their property sale. The steps, case studies, and resources in this guide will demystify the FSBO process, empowering you to make informed decisions, maximize your sale, and feel confident at each stage.

I invite you to embrace this journey as you take charge of your sale with the same independence and confidence that DIY Flex Realty stands for. You're not just selling a property—you're stepping into a role that combines financial savvy with personal agency. This book will guide you every step of the way.

PURPOSE STATEMENT

This book is designed to empower homeowners to confidently navigate the For Sale By Owner (FSBO) process, offering a comprehensive, step-by-step guide to manage every aspect of selling their property independently. For many, selling a home is one of the most significant financial and personal decisions, and by choosing FSBO, homeowners can maintain full control, save on agent commissions, and maximize profit. However, the FSBO path also comes with its unique challenges—requiring a balance of strategic planning, legal understanding, and proactive market engagement.

Through this resource, readers will find practical insights that are straightforward and actionable, enabling them to set competitive pricing, create effective marketing strategies, and confidently handle negotiations. Each chapter delves into a core component of the FSBO process, from pre-listing preparations and marketing strategies to navigating offers, closing, and post-sale considerations. With clear explanations and real-world case studies, this book breaks down complex aspects of the home-selling process, such as legal documentation, tax implications, and effective negotiation tactics, empowering sellers to approach each step with clarity and purpose.

This book serves both first-time FSBO sellers and experienced homeowners seeking a deeper understanding of the market. Whether the goal is to maximize profits, expedite the sale, or simply take full control over the process, this resource will provide the tools, templates, and knowledge essential for a successful FSBO experience. With a structured approach and comprehensive guidance, homeowners will be well-prepared to tackle the FSBO process with confidence and ensure that their sale is as profitable and smooth as possible.

In short, this guide is a reliable companion for any homeowner embarking on the FSBO journey, offering not just a roadmap but also the confidence to make informed decisions every step of the way.

TABLE OF CONTENT

INTRODUCTION

Welcome to your comprehensive guide to selling a home on your own terms. This book empowers you, the homeowner, to take charge of your property sale with confidence, leveraging a wealth of insights, strategies, and resources to navigate the For Sale By Owner (FSBO) process from start to finish. Whether you're exploring FSBO to save on commissions, maintain more control, or simply enjoy the satisfaction of doing it yourself, this guide is here to support every step of your journey.

In today's market, homeowners have access to a broad range of digital tools, data, and online platforms, making FSBO more achievable than ever before. Yet, without the support of an agent, many FSBO sellers wonder where to begin, what pitfalls to avoid, and how to make their property stand out. This book addresses these questions and more, providing structured guidance for each phase of the selling process—from setting a competitive price to managing inquiries, showings, and negotiations, all the way through to the final paperwork.

Here, you'll find:

1. Practical Insights: We'll cover real-life case studies and examples to help you understand what works, what doesn't, and how to apply these lessons to your own sale.
2. Legal and Financial Guidance: With the complexities of contracts, taxes, and compliance requirements, having a solid understanding of your obligations and opportunities is crucial. This guide simplifies legal aspects and provides direction on when and how to consult a professional.

3. Marketing and Exposure Tips: Selling a property requires more than listing it online. This guide covers strategies for making your listing stand out, using both traditional and digital channels to maximize visibility and appeal.

4. Tools and Resources: You'll find checklists, templates, and links to online tools to streamline your workflow and keep everything organized.

This book is designed for homeowners at all levels—whether it's your first FSBO experience or you're a seasoned seller looking to refine your approach. By following this roadmap, you'll gain a clear, actionable path to a successful sale and maximize your return on investment.

Selling your home on your own is an exciting and rewarding endeavor. You're in control of the process, the decisions, and the outcome. With the right knowledge and preparation, you can turn a potentially complex process into a straightforward and fulfilling achievement. Let's get started on making your FSBO journey a success!

CHAPTER 1
INTRODUCTION TO FSBO (FOR SALE BY OWNER)

1. Fsbo: Introduction To For Sale By Owner

FSBO, or "For Sale By Owner," is a method where homeowners sell their property independently, bypassing traditional real estate agents. This approach empowers sellers to handle the entire selling process themselves, from pricing the property and marketing it to negotiating with buyers and finalizing the sale. By opting for FSBO, sellers have the chance to save on real estate agent commissions, which typically amount to 5-6% of the sale price, allowing them to retain more of the proceeds (National Association of Realtors, 2023). This method appeals to sellers looking to maximize their profit margins, especially in a strong real estate market. However, FSBO requires a solid understanding of the selling process, market dynamics, and legal requirements. FSBO is ideal for sellers who feel confident managing the process and who are prepared to invest time and effort in tasks typically handled by a real estate professional.

2. Characteristics Of An Fsbo-Ready Seller

Not every seller is suited for FSBO, as it requires specific skills and qualities to navigate the complexities of the sale. The following traits align well with FSBO success:

- Organized and Detail-Oriented: FSBO sellers must manage paperwork, schedules, and requirements meticulously.

- Comfortable with Negotiation: Since FSBO sellers negotiate directly with buyers, strong negotiation skills are essential for achieving favorable terms.
- Market Savvy: Understanding local market dynamics helps sellers set competitive prices, recognize serious offers, and assess buyer interest (NAR, 2023; Real Estate Marketing Insights, 2023).
- Strong Communication Skills: FSBO sellers should feel comfortable communicating with buyers, inspectors, and attorneys to ensure a smooth transaction.
- Time Availability and Flexibility: FSBO sellers need dedicated time for showings, inquiries, and follow-ups.
- Willingness to Learn: FSBO involves a learning curve, and sellers open to researching the steps involved are more likely to succeed.
- Realistic Expectations for Sale Time: FSBO homes may take longer to sell than agent-listed properties, so realistic timelines are essential.
- Awareness of Buyer Reluctance: Some buyers may be wary of FSBO properties, so sellers should proactively address concerns by preparing thorough documentation and considering pre-sale inspections (Real Estate Research Institute, 2022).
- Financial Preparedness: While FSBO can save on commissions, selling independently may involve costs for listing, photography, legal consultation, or closing fees. A budget helps avoid surprises.

FSBO can be a rewarding option for sellers who possess these qualities and are prepared for the responsibilities involved.

FSBO Statistics

According to the National Association of Realtors (NAR), approximately 7% of U.S. home sales are FSBO transactions. This figure represents a smaller segment of the market, but FSBO remains attractive to homeowners motivated to maximize net proceeds by avoiding agent commissions (NAR, 2023). FSBO is especially appealing for sellers with a strong understanding of their local market who want direct control over the transaction. However, FSBO properties often sell at lower median prices than agent-assisted sales, primarily due to limited marketing reach and buyer access (NAR, 2023; Zillow Research, 2023). FSBO requires sellers to take on responsibilities typically managed by real estate professionals, including property pricing, marketing, negotiation, and legal paperwork. For sellers with the motivation and skills to handle these tasks, FSBO can be a viable and worthwhile choice.

3. Differences Between Fsbo And Using A Traditional Real Estate Agent

Marketing Reach: Real estate agents have access to the Multiple Listing Service (MLS), a database that connects listings to a vast network of agents and buyers, providing high visibility across platforms. This reach is essential for attracting a broad pool of potential buyers, potentially leading to more competitive offers and a quicker sale (NAR, 2023). FSBO sellers do not have direct MLS access unless they use a flat-fee MLS service, which allows them to list on the MLS for a one-time fee. Without this, FSBO sellers must rely on alternative methods, such as free or paid listings on Zillow, Craigslist, Redfin, and Facebook Marketplace (Zillow Research, 2023; Redfin Insights, 2022). While these platforms can attract buyer traffic, they may not offer the comprehensive exposure that MLS listings provide, potentially limiting the buyer pool.

Marketing Resources: Real estate agents often offer professional marketing strategies like photography, virtual tours, open houses, social media ads, and email campaigns. FSBO sellers may need to take on these tasks independently or hire professionals for key services, such as photography or virtual tours, to create a compelling listing (Real Estate Marketing Insights, 2023).

Negotiation and Legal Support: In an agent-assisted sale, the agent handles negotiations and legal requirements. FSBO sellers must navigate these aspects alone, which requires negotiation skills and familiarity with legal and contract requirements. Real estate attorneys or legal professionals can offer guidance to FSBO sellers, helping ensure all legalities are managed effectively (Fiverr Freelance Services, 2023; Real Estate Legal Guide, 2023).

4. Homeowner's Role And Responsibilities In Fsbo

FSBO sellers are responsible for every aspect of the sale, including:

- Setting a Competitive Price: Conducting a Comparative Market Analysis (CMA) to determine the property's market value.
- Marketing the Property: Creating listings, preparing photos, conducting showings, and responding to inquiries.
- Handling Showings: Scheduling and managing property tours and open houses.
- Negotiating with Buyers: Managing price negotiations and other terms with buyers or their agents.
- Managing Paperwork and Legalities: Preparing disclosure forms, sales contracts, and navigating state requirements (Real Estate Legal Guide, 2023).

FSBO sellers must be organized, resourceful, and prepared to invest time in each of these steps to ensure a successful sale.

5. When Fsbo Might Be The Best Choice

FSBO can be a strong choice in certain situations, such as:

- Strong Seller's Market: High demand may reduce the need for agent support, as buyers actively seek properties.

- Lower-Value Properties: For lower-priced homes, commission costs may be disproportionately high, making FSBO attractive (NAR, 2023).
- Prior Real Estate Experience: Sellers familiar with the transaction process may feel comfortable managing the sale independently.
- Desire for Control: FSBO is ideal for sellers who want full control over pricing, marketing, and transaction terms.

Identifying these scenarios helps readers assess if FSBO aligns with their goals and circumstances.

REAL-WORLD FSBO CASE STUDIES

Case Study 1:

FSBO Success in a Competitive Market

Overview:

Emily, a homeowner in a competitive seller's market, listed her $300,000 home using FSBO to avoid commission fees. Confident in her knowledge of local market trends, Emily listed her property on Zillow and Facebook Marketplace (Zillow Research, 2023). Though she faced challenges managing showings and paperwork, she proactively addressed buyer concerns and maintained flexible showing hours, which led to multiple offers.

Outcome:

Emily sold her home within 30 days, saving an estimated $10,000 in commissions. Handling the closing paperwork posed unexpected challenges, so she hired a real estate attorney to finalize the sale (Real Estate Legal Guide, 2023).

Lessons Learned:

Emily's FSBO experience demonstrated the value of strong market knowledge, proactive buyer communication, and professional assistance with paperwork.

Case Study 2: FSBO Challenges in a Slower Market

Overview:

- Robert, a homeowner in a buyer's market, chose FSBO to avoid agent commissions. After 60 days with limited interest, he hired an appraiser, adjusted his price, and offered a buyer's agent commission.

Outcome:

- Robert sold his property after these adjustments, though he incurred appraisal and buyer's agent commission costs (Real Estate Marketing Insights, 2023). His experience highlighted the importance of market awareness and pricing flexibility in a slower market.

Lessons Learned:

- FSBO in a slower market may require strategic pricing adjustments and budget allocation for professional support.

Common Pitfalls in FSBO Sales and Solutions

Pitfall 1: Pricing Errors One of the most common pitfalls FSBO sellers face is setting an incorrect listing price. Overpricing a property can result in it sitting on the market for extended periods, deterring potential buyers and possibly leading to price cuts, which may appear as desperation. Conversely, underpricing can mean leaving money on the table. Emotional attachment to the property can also lead to inflated expectations about its worth, making objective pricing a challenge.

Solution: To set a realistic, competitive price, FSBO sellers should conduct a Comparative Market Analysis (CMA) using online tools or real estate websites that show recent comparable sales (Zillow Research, 2023). However, because CMAs can be complex, many FSBO sellers benefit from hiring a local appraiser for a professional evaluation, providing an unbiased estimate of the home's market value. By setting an informed price based on market conditions rather than emotion, sellers can better attract serious buyers and avoid the costly consequences of mispricing.

Pitfall 2: Limited Market Reach

FSBO sellers often lack access to the same marketing tools as real estate agents, most notably the Multiple Listing Service (MLS), which is essential for broad exposure. Limited visibility means the property may only reach a fraction of the buyer pool, resulting in fewer inquiries and less competitive offers (NAR, 2023).

Solution:

To maximize reach, FSBO sellers can pay for a flat-fee MLS listing, allowing their property to appear in MLS searches without hiring a full-service agent. Additionally, leveraging multiple online platforms—such as Zillow, Craigslist, Redfin, and social media channels like Facebook Marketplace—can help capture buyer interest (Redfin Insights, 2022; Zillow Research, 2023). Creating a professional, engaging listing is essential; this includes using high-quality photos, providing a detailed and appealing description, and highlighting unique property features. For added impact, FSBO sellers can consider hiring a professional photographer or videographer to create a virtual tour, increasing the likelihood of catching potential buyers' attention.

Pitfall 3:

Handling Legal and Paperwork Requirements Navigating the legal and paperwork requirements in a real estate transaction can be overwhelming for FSBO sellers, as real estate contracts are complex and vary widely by state. Errors or omissions in disclosure forms, title documents, or sales contracts can lead to legal liabilities, delays, or even jeopardize the sale altogether. Many states also require specific disclosure forms, such as those regarding lead paint, property condition, and known defects, which FSBO sellers must handle with care to remain compliant with local laws (Real Estate Legal Guide, 2023).

Solution:

It's strongly recommended that FSBO sellers consult with a real estate attorney or a title company to review all legal documents, verify compliance with state regulations, and guide them through the required paperwork. Legal professionals can provide clarity on contract terms, ensure accurate completion of disclosure forms, and address specific legalities, such as transfer taxes and closing costs, that could otherwise be missed. For FSBO sellers on a budget, platforms like Fiverr offer freelance services where sellers can find experienced real estate attorneys, paralegals, or legal consultants for contract reviews or guidance at more affordable rates (Fiverr Freelance Services, 2023). However, given the high stakes of real estate transactions, it's advisable to verify the qualifications and experience of any professional consulted on Fiverr or similar sites. While professional assistance may come with additional costs, working with an attorney or legal expert provides invaluable peace of mind, reduces the risk of costly mistakes, and ensures a smoother transaction overall.

FSBO Checklist for Chapter 1:

You can take actionable steps to ensure you're prepared for a successful For Sale By Owner sale. Here's how to approach each item on the list:

1. Evaluate Motivation for FSBO

- Action: Write down specific reasons for choosing FSBO. Examples might include saving on commission fees, having control over the sale, or leveraging personal knowledge of the property.
- Calculate Potential Savings: Estimate what you could save by not paying a traditional agent commission. Multiply your expected sale price by 5-6% to see what you're likely to save, and compare this with any anticipated FSBO-related costs, such as marketing or legal fees.

2. Research Market Trends

- Action: Use online tools like Zillow, Realtor.com, or Redfin to find recent comparable home sales (known as "comps") in your area. Focus on homes similar to yours in size, location, and features.
- Assess Demand and Seasonality: Take note of how quickly homes are selling and at what prices. If it's a high-demand season (like spring and early summer), you may need less intensive marketing. If it's slower, adjust your expectations and consider pricing accordingly.

3. Prepare Essential Documents

- Action: Research your state's disclosure requirements. This often includes forms like property condition reports, lead paint disclosure (if built before 1978), and details on any known defects.

- Gather Contracts: Obtain a standard real estate sales contract for your state. If needed, consult an attorney or use online sources to ensure compliance.
- Organize Financial Agreements: Prepare any loan payoff information, HOA documents (if applicable), and other financial paperwork. Having these ready ensures a smooth closing.

4. Determine Your Marketing Strategy

- Action: Decide if you'll use paid options (like flat-fee MLS services) or free platforms (such as Zillow or Facebook Marketplace). Paid MLS access provides more visibility, while free platforms keep costs down but may take longer to generate leads.
- Create a Professional Listing: Invest time or hire help to take high-quality photos and craft a compelling description of your property. Highlight unique features or recent upgrades that make your property stand out.

5. Establish a Network for Assistance

- Action: Identify professionals who can help with the sale, such as a real estate attorney (for legal paperwork) and an appraiser (for pricing). Reach out to them early to discuss fees and availability.
- Consider Freelance Resources: If you're on a budget, platforms like Fiverr or Upwork can be helpful for finding affordable marketing or legal assistance. Make sure to verify the credentials and experience of any freelancers you hire.

Next Steps

This checklist acts as a roadmap to get you prepared. By completing each task, you'll be better equipped to handle the FSBO process and make informed decisions. As you work through each item, you'll gain clarity on your market, set up the legal and marketing foundations, and create a support network for any complex issues.

References

National Association of Realtors. (2023). *2023 profile of home buyers and sellers*. National Association of Realtors. Retrieved from https://www.nar.realtor/research-and-statistics

Real Estate Marketing Insights. (2023). The essentials of effective FSBO marketing. Real Estate Marketing Insights. Retrieved from https://www.realestatemarketinginsights.com

Real Estate Research Institute. (2022). Common FSBO buyer hesitations and how to address them. Real Estate Research Institute. Retrieved from https://www.reri.org

Zillow Research. (2023). FSBO trends and statistics in the U.S. market. Zillow Research. Retrieved from https://www.zillow.com/research

Redfin Insights. (2022). Alternatives to traditional MLS listings: Flat-fee and FSBO strategies. Redfin Insights. Retrieved from https://www.redfin.com/news

Real Estate Legal Guide. (2023). FSBO legal considerations: Navigating contracts and disclosures without an agent. Real Estate Legal Guide. Retrieved from https://www.realestatelegalguide.com

Fiverr Freelance Services. (2023). Hiring legal and real estate experts on a budget. Fiverr. Retrieved from https://www.fiverr.com

CHAPTER 2
FSBO BENEFITS AND CHALLENGES

1. Cost Savings And Comparative Financial Impact

One of the primary motivations for homeowners choosing the FSBO model is the potential for substantial cost savings, particularly by avoiding the traditional real estate agent commission fees. Real estate agents generally charge between 5-6% of the final sale price as commission, which for a $300,000 home translates to $15,000 to $18,000 (National Association of Realtors, 2023). This significant amount, which otherwise goes to an agent, can be retained by the seller and reallocated to enhance the property's appeal or address essential selling expenses, such as marketing, staging, or legal consultations (Zillow Research, 2023).

However, while FSBO can eliminate agent fees, sellers must account for other costs to gain a full picture of the financial impact and determine whether FSBO aligns with their budget and objectives. Below is a breakdown of typical FSBO-related expenses and how sellers can strategically manage them to maximize net profit.

Breakdown of Typical FSBO-Related Costs

FSBO sellers should consider the following common expenses when preparing to list their property:

1. Flat-Fee MLS Listings: To gain access to the Multiple Listing Service (MLS), which dramatically increases exposure, many FSBO sellers opt for a flat-fee MLS listing. Costs for this ser-

vice vary, typically ranging from $100 to $500, depending on the provider and the features included (Real Estate Marketing Insights, 2023).

2. Professional Photography and Videography: High-quality visuals are essential in today's competitive real estate market. Professional photos generally cost between $200 and $500, while videography or virtual tours can range from $300 to $1,000, depending on the size and layout of the property (Redfin Insights, 2022).

3. Staging: Professional staging can enhance the property's appeal and help prospective buyers envision themselves living there. Staging fees can vary significantly but usually range from $500 to $2,500, depending on the level of service and duration of the listing (NAR, 2023).

4. Targeted Advertising: To reach a broader audience, FSBO sellers might invest in digital advertising on platforms such as Zillow, Facebook Marketplace, or local real estate websites. These ads can cost between $50 and $300 per month, depending on the scope of the campaign (Zillow Research, 2023).

5. Legal Consultation: Real estate transactions require careful attention to legal details, such as disclosures, contracts, and compliance with state regulations. Hiring a real estate attorney to review documents generally costs between $500 and $1,500, though costs may vary based on location and specific needs (Real Estate Legal Guide, 2023).

6. Appraisal and Inspection: Some FSBO sellers opt to invest in a pre-listing appraisal or home inspection to accurately price the property and identify potential issues. These services typically cost between $300 and $700 each but can help avoid costly mistakes later (Zillow Research, 2023).

7. Miscellaneous Fees: Other potential costs include open house supplies, lockboxes, yard signs, and online listing fees. While

these items may seem small individually, they can add up, typically costing between $100 and $300.

Strategic Allocation of Savings

The money saved by avoiding agent commissions can be strategically reinvested into the FSBO process to enhance the property's appeal, attract more buyers, and ultimately secure a higher sale price. Sellers can consider the following strategies to make the most of their savings:

- Marketing Investment: Allocating funds towards a robust marketing strategy can improve listing visibility and increase buyer interest. By budgeting for professional photography, a flat-fee MLS listing, and targeted online ads, sellers can significantly increase their reach without the need for an agent's network.

- Home Improvements and Staging: FSBO sellers often find it beneficial to reinvest some of their commission savings into home improvements or staging, especially if the property has outdated features. Research shows that even small upgrades—such as fresh paint, landscaping, or minor renovations—can yield high returns on investment and make the home more attractive to buyers (Real Estate Marketing Insights, 2023).

- Legal Assurance: Setting aside funds for a real estate attorney ensures compliance with state regulations and reduces the risk of legal issues, which can be costly if not addressed properly. Consulting a professional helps streamline the transaction and ensures all required disclosures are accurately presented.

Comparative Financial Analysis

To fully understand the financial impact of FSBO, sellers should conduct a comparative analysis, taking into account both the money saved on commissions and any necessary FSBO-related expenses. This analysis helps sellers evaluate the financial feasibility of FSBO based on their specific property value, location, and market conditions. Here's how a sample calculation might look for a property valued at $300,000:

Expense	Cost Range
Agent Commission (5-6%)	$15,000 - $18,000 (Saved)
Flat-Fee MLS Listing	$100 - $500
Professional Photography	$200 - $500
Videography/Virtual Tour	$300 - $1,000
Staging	$500 - $2,500
Targeted Advertising	$50 - $300/month
Legal Consultation	$500 - $1,500
Pre-Listing Appraisal/Inspection	$300 - $700 each
Miscellaneous Fees	$100 - $300
Total Potential Expenses	$2,050 - $7,600
Total Net Savings	$7,400 - $15,950

In this example, the seller could potentially save between $7,400 and $15,950 by choosing FSBO, depending on the specific expenses incurred.

Financial Planning Tips for FSBO Sellers

To ensure the FSBO process is financially advantageous, sellers should follow these financial planning tips:

1. Create a Detailed Budget: Outline all potential FSBO-related costs, and allocate funds based on your property's specific needs. This will help avoid unexpected expenses and give you a clear picture of your potential savings.
2. Prioritize Key Investments: Consider which services are essential for your listing. If your home is located in a high-demand area, it may need less advertising. However, in slower markets, it's worthwhile to allocate a larger portion of your budget to staging and digital marketing.
3. Track Expenses Diligently: Keep receipts and track all expenses throughout the FSBO process to ensure you stay within budget and can accurately calculate your final savings.
4. Consult with a Financial Advisor: For high-value properties, a financial advisor can provide guidance on tax implications and ensure the FSBO approach aligns with your financial goals.

Summary

While FSBO offers the advantage of saving on commission fees, sellers should be prepared for additional costs associated with marketing, legal consultations, and home improvements. By conducting a comprehensive financial analysis, FSBO sellers can better understand the impact of these expenses and make informed decisions that maximize their overall savings and net profit.

CASE STUDY 1: STRATEGIC COST MANAGEMENT IN FSBO

Overview:

David, a homeowner in a well-populated suburban neighborhood, decided to pursue the FSBO route to save on the $20,000 commission fee he would have paid to a traditional real estate agent. His home, a three-bedroom property in good condition, was located in an area with moderately high demand but where professional real estate listings were the norm. Aware that he would be competing with agent-listed properties, David recognized the need to make his home as appealing and visible as possible without exceeding his limited budget.

David allocated a budget of $3,000 to cover essential FSBO-related expenses, including a flat-fee MLS listing for $400, professional photography for $250, and legal assistance for $800. This left him with $1,550 for other key costs, such as online advertising and minor home improvements. David carefully researched each expense, prioritizing services that would enhance his property's visibility and curb appeal.

Challenges and Strategies:

David faced several challenges during the FSBO process, including:

1. Limited Market Exposure: Without an agent's network, David was concerned about reaching enough buyers. To address this, he purchased a flat-fee MLS listing to gain access to the MLS database, thereby allowing his listing to appear on widely used platforms like Zillow and Realtor.com. This MLS access helped him reach a broader audience without a full-service agent.

2. Visual Appeal: Understanding that professional photos were essential to attract buyers online, David hired a photographer who specialized in real estate and paid close attention to the lighting, angles, and overall presentation of each room. The photographer suggested minor staging techniques, such as rearranging furniture and decluttering, to make the home appear more spacious and inviting. This initial investment of $250 in high-quality visuals helped his listing stand out, even among agent-represented properties.

3. Legal and Compliance Concerns: David was also apprehensive about managing the legal requirements, particularly around disclosures and contracts. He hired a real estate attorney for $800 to review his contracts, prepare necessary disclosures, and ensure compliance with state regulations. This decision gave David confidence in navigating the legal aspects and reduced the likelihood of errors that could delay the sale or cause legal complications later.

4. Competing in a Traditional Market: Since most homes in his area were agent-listed, David knew he would need to market aggressively. He allocated $300 to digital advertising, running targeted ads on Facebook and local real estate websites. These ads highlighted his home's unique features, such as a newly renovated kitchen and spacious backyard, which were major selling points in his neighborhood. By managing his ad campaigns closely, David was able to drive considerable traffic to his listing without overspending.

5. Time Management and Flexibility: Balancing FSBO responsibilities with his day job was another challenge for David. To manage inquiries and showings efficiently, he set specific times for open houses and created a system to track interested buyers. David used online tools to streamline appointment scheduling, allowing him to optimize his time and accommodate multiple viewings over weekends.

Outcome:

David's home attracted a steady flow of prospective buyers thanks to his well-prepared listing and targeted advertising. Within 45 days, he received a competitive offer close to his asking price. His total FSBO-related expenses amounted to approximately $3,000, leaving him with around $17,000 in net savings compared to selling through an agent. The combination of MLS visibility, high-quality photography, and professional legal guidance contributed significantly to his successful sale.

Lessons Learned:

David's experience highlights several key takeaways for FSBO sellers:

- Strategic Budgeting: A carefully planned budget allowed David to allocate funds to high-impact areas, such as MLS access, professional visuals, and legal support, which enhanced his listing's visibility and credibility.
- Quality Over Quantity in Marketing: By investing in professional photography and targeted online advertising, David was able to attract serious buyers and compete effectively with agent-listed properties in his area. His focus on quality made his listing stand out in a crowded market.
- Importance of Legal Assurance: Hiring a real estate attorney provided David with the peace of mind and legal accuracy needed to manage a successful FSBO transaction. This investment minimized risks and helped him avoid costly mistakes.
- Effective Time Management: Balancing FSBO tasks with personal responsibilities is a common challenge for sellers. David's use of scheduling tools and pre-planned open house times helped him manage inquiries and showings efficiently, allowing him to maintain a professional presentation despite his busy schedule.

In summary, David's case illustrates that FSBO can be a financially viable and successful option with thorough planning and disciplined budgeting. His experience underscores that targeted investments in marketing, legal assistance, and time management can have a significant positive impact on the sale outcome, maximizing the financial benefits of the FSBO model.

Case Study 2:

High-End FSBO with Major Savings

Overview: Jenny, who owned a high-end property in a competitive market, went FSBO to save nearly $50,000 in commissions. She allocated $7,000 to create a professional listing, including 3D virtual tours, high-quality photos, and professional staging services.

Outcome: Jenny's property sold in three weeks for the asking price. By investing in premium marketing, she captured buyer attention quickly and saved a significant amount by not paying commission fees.

Lessons Learned: Jenny's experience shows that high-end FSBOs can be successful with appropriate investments in professional-grade marketing materials, which can yield competitive offers without an agent.

2. Control Over The Process

One of FSBO's most appealing aspects is the autonomy it offers. Sellers have complete control over every aspect of the sale, from pricing and listing creation to managing showings and negotiating with buyers. This freedom enables sellers to make timely adjustments, such as modifying the listing description or price based on market feedback, without needing agent input or approval (Redfin Insights, 2022). For many, this independence provides the flexibility to tailor marketing strategies and emphasize unique property features to attract buyers.

Additionally, FSBO allows sellers to experiment with dynamic pricing strategies. Without an agent's involvement, sellers can respond to buyer interest, seasonal trends, or neighborhood market changes and adjust prices accordingly. However, managing the sale independently requires a strong understanding of local market trends, effective negotiation strategies, and familiarity with real estate laws (NAR, 2023).

Case Study 3: Leveraging FSBO Control for a Tailored Marketing Approach

Overview:

Sarah, a former real estate agent, chose FSBO to maintain control over her home sale, especially as she was experienced in local market trends. She tailored her listing to highlight features that were particularly attractive in her area and adjusted her pricing strategy based on buyer feedback.

Outcome:

Sarah sold her home within 30 days. Her expertise enabled her to make real-time adjustments to the listing, refine her negotiation approach, and optimize her pricing strategy, resulting in a smooth and profitable sale.

Lessons Learned:

Sarah's case emphasizes that FSBO can be highly beneficial for those with real estate knowledge who prefer a hands-on approach, particularly when adapting to buyer needs and market demands.

3. Setting The Right Price

Determining the right price requires more than simply matching the latest sale price of a nearby home. FSBO sellers need to consider recent market trends, target buyer demographics, and unique property features to appeal to the most likely buyers.

Additional Considerations

- Historical Pricing Trends: Analyzing how property values have changed over the past few years gives insight into the market's stability and long-term trends. Understanding these trends helps sellers set realistic expectations and price their property accordingly.

- Pricing for Different Buyer Types: Tailoring pricing to the target buyer (e.g., first-time buyers, investors, luxury homebuyers) can improve a property's appeal. For instance, investors may focus on appreciation and rental potential, while first-time buyers might look for affordability and amenities.

Case Study 1: Competitive Market Pricing

Overview:

Rebecca, a homeowner in a high-demand neighborhood, chose to sell her property as a FSBO to avoid paying agent commissions. With her neighborhood experiencing consistent buyer interest and an average annual property value increase of 10%, she knew there would be strong demand. Before setting her price, Rebecca conducted a thorough analysis of local pricing trends, reviewed recent comparable sales, and paid close attention to properties similar in size, layout, and condition.

Rebecca observed that comparable homes in her area were often selling above list price but also noticed that homes with minor pricing flexibility seemed to attract more initial buyer interest. Wanting to position her home as an attractive option, she decided to set her price slightly below similar listings, strategically aiming to spark interest and create a sense of urgency.

Strategy and Execution:

1. Research and Data Collection: Rebecca examined local market trends using various online real estate platforms and kept an eye on neighborhood listings and sales. She also analyzed factors such as average days on market and typical price reductions (if any) in her area.

2. Pricing Decision: Based on her findings, she decided to price her property approximately 3-5% below the closest comparable listings, which she believed would attract a higher volume of potential buyers and set her property apart.

3. Marketing and Presentation: Rebecca emphasized her pricing strategy in her listing description, subtly noting that the property was "competitively priced for a quick sale in a sought-after neighborhood." She hired a professional photographer to showcase her property's best features, adding curb appeal and high-quality interior photos to make her listing as visually attractive as possible.

4. Open House and Buyer Engagement: Rebecca held an open house over the weekend following her listing's release, inviting interested buyers to view the property and feel the competitive pressure from other potential buyers firsthand. By scheduling all viewings on the same day, she created a busy, high-interest environment.

Outcome:

Rebecca's approach to setting her price slightly below similar listings paid off. Within a week, she received multiple offers. Due to the high level of buyer interest, a few potential buyers submitted offers above the asking price to strengthen their positions. By the end of the week, Rebecca was able to choose an offer well above her original list price, allowing her to secure a sale that exceeded her initial expectations.

Lesson Learned:

Rebecca's case illustrates that in a competitive market, pricing slightly below comparable listings can stimulate immediate buyer interest, leading to a bidding environment. This strategy can ultimately drive up the final sale price, achieving results similar to—or even exceeding—those of properties initially listed higher. Additionally, her approach highlights the importance of research and preparation in pricing, showing that setting an attractive price, creating an appealing listing, and facilitating a sense of competition can help maximize a property's sale outcome.

Case Study 2: Tailoring Pricing to First-Time Buyers

Overview:

Laura owned a cozy starter home in a suburban neighborhood popular with first-time buyers. Known for its affordability, proximity to local schools, and family-friendly atmosphere, the area frequently attracted young professionals and couples looking to buy their first property. Recognizing the unique appeal of her home to budget-conscious buyers, Laura decided to take a tailored approach to her pricing strategy.

After studying recent sales data for similar properties, Laura found that comparable homes were typically priced around the neighborhood median. To differentiate her home and offer clear value, she opted to set her price slightly below this median, positioning her home as a more affordable entry into the market. Her goal was to attract serious first-time buyers and encourage faster offers by creating a strong value proposition.

Strategy and Execution:

1. Research and Demographic Targeting: Laura analyzed data on recent buyers in her area and noted that the majority were first-time buyers. By reviewing sales data on nearby homes and tracking their time on market, she identified a median price range for her home type.

2. Pricing Below the Median: Rather than matching comparable prices, Laura listed her home about 2-3% below the area median for similar properties. This slight reduction was designed to appeal to first-time buyers who might be stretching their budgets to make their first purchase. Her pricing also aimed

to position her home as a "value buy" compared to competing listings.

3. Enhanced Marketing for First-Time Buyers: Laura crafted her listing description to highlight features often valued by first-time buyers, such as the home's move-in-ready condition, proximity to public transportation, and low maintenance costs. She also emphasized the home's affordability, noting that it was "an ideal starter home at an unbeatable price."

4. Leveraging Online Platforms and Social Media: Knowing that first-time buyers often start their searches online, Laura focused her marketing on digital platforms popular with younger buyers. She used Zillow, Facebook Marketplace, and local community groups to increase visibility among her target demographic, ensuring the home reached first-time buyers actively looking in her area.

Outcome:

Laura's pricing and marketing strategy succeeded in creating a strong attraction for first-time buyers. Within the first two weeks, she received multiple offers from buyers eager to enter the market. Her competitive pricing strategy led to heightened buyer interest, and she was able to accept an offer at her asking price quickly, with minimal time on the market.

Lesson Learned:

Laura's experience demonstrates the value of pricing with the buyer demographic in mind. By setting her price slightly below the median, she effectively targeted budget-conscious first-time buyers and created a sense of urgency that helped her close the sale quickly. This case highlights the importance of understanding the needs and constraints of specific buyer groups, showing that tailoring the pricing and marketing strategy to the demographic most likely to purchase can lead to faster sales and a smoother selling experience.

4. Potential Challenges And Solutions

Challenge 1: Limited Exposure

FSBO sellers often struggle with limited visibility due to a lack of access to the Multiple Listing Service (MLS), which is a primary tool for agent-listed properties to gain wide exposure. Without MLS access, FSBO listings may not reach as many potential buyers, leading to fewer offers and a potentially longer sale time (NAR, 2023).

Solution:

FSBO sellers can expand their reach by purchasing a flat-fee MLS listing to appear in MLS searches, increasing exposure without hiring a full-service agent. In addition, leveraging online platforms—such as Zillow, Redfin, Craigslist, and Facebook Marketplace—can help attract buyers. Using professional photography, high-quality descriptions, and even virtual tours can further enhance the listing's appeal (Zillow Research, 2023; Redfin Insights, 2022).

Challenge 2: Negotiation and Legal Complexity

Negotiating directly with buyers and managing legal paperwork can be daunting for FSBO sellers. Real estate contracts vary by state, and without an agent, sellers may miss important disclosures, such as lead paint or known defects, which can expose them to legal liabilities (Real Estate Legal Guide, 2023).

Solution:

To mitigate these risks, FSBO sellers should consult with a real estate attorney for a comprehensive document review. Sellers on a budget can also explore online freelance platforms like Fiverr, which provide access to experienced legal professionals at various price points (Fiverr Freelance Services, 2023). Working with a legal expert ensures accuracy in disclosures and contracts, reducing the chances of costly mistakes.

Challenge 3: Accurate Pricing

Setting an accurate price is critical to attract serious buyers and close a sale efficiently. FSBO sellers without agent support may struggle with price setting, as emotional attachment can cloud objectivity. Over-pricing can deter buyers, while underpricing might reduce the seller's profit (Real Estate Marketing Insights, 2023).

Solution:

FSBO sellers can perform a Comparative Market Analysis (CMA) using tools like Zillow's price estimate or hire an appraiser for a professional valuation. These approaches help set a realistic and competitive price, ultimately improving the listing's appeal and expediting the sale process (Zillow Research, 2023).

Case Study 4:

Pricing for Success in FSBO

Overview:

Mark, a first-time FSBO seller, initially overestimated his property's value. After several weeks without offers, he researched comparable homes and consulted a local appraiser for an objective valuation.

Outcome:

By adjusting the price based on market data, Mark increased buyer interest, and the property sold within a week of the adjustment.

Lessons Learned:

Mark's experience underscores the value of accurate pricing in FSBO and the importance of basing price adjustments on market data rather than emotional bias.

Conclusion

The FSBO model can yield substantial benefits, such as cost savings and complete control over the sales process. However, it also requires significant commitment, knowledge of the market, and careful planning. For sellers who are prepared to manage every aspect of the transaction, from budgeting and marketing to negotiation and legal compliance, FSBO can be a rewarding alternative to agent-assisted sales. By leveraging resources like flat-fee MLS listings, freelance legal services, and professional appraisals, FSBO sellers can navigate common challenges effectively and maximize the potential benefits of selling independently.

Suggested APA References for Chapter 2

National Association of Realtors. (2023). 2023 profile of home buyers and sellers. National Association of Realtors. Retrieved from https://www.nar.realtor/research-and-statistics

Real Estate Marketing Insights. (2023). Financial planning for FSBO sellers: Beyond commission savings. Real Estate Marketing Insights. Retrieved from https://www.realestatemarketinginsights.com

Redfin Insights. (2022). Pros and cons of FSBO listings: What sellers need to know. Redfin Insights. Retrieved from https://www.redfin.com/news

Real Estate Legal Guide. (2023). Navigating legal complexities in FSBO sales: Contracts, disclosures, and compliance. Real Estate Legal Guide. Retrieved from https://www.realestatelegalguide.com

Zillow Research. (2023). Strategies for effective FSBO pricing and marketing. Zillow Research. Retrieved from https://www.zillow.com/research

Fiverr Freelance Services. (2023). Cost-effective legal consultations for FSBO sellers. Fiverr. Retrieved from https://www.fiverr.com

CHAPTER 3
ADVANCED PRICING STRATEGY

Setting the right price is one of the most critical steps in a successful FSBO sale. A well-planned pricing strategy attracts buyers, reduces time on the market, and maximizes profitability. This chapter dives into key strategies for setting the right price, using pricing tools, avoiding common pitfalls, and provides real-world case studies to guide FSBO sellers.

1. Advanced Pricing Models And Tools

Using different pricing models and tools can help FSBO sellers set a competitive, data-driven price that aligns with their sale objectives, whether aiming for a quick sale or maximum profit.

In-Depth Pricing Models

- Psychological Pricing: Setting a price just below a major threshold (e.g., $299,000 instead of $300,000) can make a property feel more affordable and attract buyers who may be filtering listings by price.
- Anchor Pricing: In markets with varying property values, anchoring a property's price near higher-priced homes can create a sense of value. This approach is especially effective in neighborhoods with a mix of luxury and mid-range homes.

Pricing Tool Best Practices

- Using AVMs (Automated Valuation Models) Wisely: Tools like Zillow's Zestimate and Redfin's Estimate provide initial figures but may lack accuracy for local nuances. Sellers should use these as rough estimates and validate them with a Comparative Market Analysis (CMA) or a professional appraisal.
- Creating a Pricing Dashboard: Using a spreadsheet or digital tool to monitor comparable sales, neighborhood trends, and buyer interest over time can help sellers adjust prices promptly based on data insights.

CASE STUDY 3: USING ANCHOR PRICING TO HIGHLIGHT VALUE

Overview:

John owned a mid-sized home in an upscale neighborhood characterized by a mix of property values, with larger, high-priced homes nearby. Given the neighborhood's desirability and affluent demographic, most listings were at premium price points. John's home, while attractive, was slightly smaller and lacked some of the high-end finishes and additional amenities found in neighboring properties. To stand out in this competitive environment, John adopted an anchor pricing strategy.

Instead of matching his property with similarly priced listings in the area, he chose to set his asking price slightly below the higher-priced homes around him. This approach was intended to create a perception of value, positioning his home as an affordable yet desirable option within an upscale market. John's goal was to attract buyers looking to enter this prestigious neighborhood but who were sensitive to the high price tags of nearby properties.

Strategy and Execution:

1. Market Research and Comparative Pricing: John reviewed recent sales data and identified a pricing range for upscale homes in the area. He noticed that the largest and most feature-rich homes were priced around 10-15% higher than what he initially intended for his listing. By positioning his home as a more accessible option, John could use the higher prices of neighboring properties as an anchor, making his home look like a good deal by comparison.

2. Setting an Anchored Price Point: John priced his property approximately 7% below the nearest high-priced comparable homes. This pricing offered a middle ground, appealing to buyers who wanted to live in the area but couldn't justify the top-tier prices. His anchored price point also created an impression of potential value, as buyers could see they were getting the benefit of the location without the premium associated with larger homes.

3. Emphasizing Value in Marketing: John crafted his listing to highlight both the features of his home and the advantages of its location. He used phrases like "affordable luxury" and "exceptional value in a premier neighborhood" to emphasize the deal his home represented relative to nearby high-priced properties. He also highlighted its proximity to top schools, shopping, and dining options, which were key selling points for buyers in this neighborhood.

4. Creating a Targeted Sales Strategy: John targeted his marketing towards buyers who wanted to break into the neighborhood without paying the highest prices. He strategically listed his property on upscale real estate platforms and worked with local agents who specialized in upscale properties, positioning his home as the best value among listings in the area.

Outcome:

John's anchored pricing strategy attracted significant interest from buyers who viewed his property as a rare find in an otherwise high-priced market. By positioning his home below the top-end properties, John created a perception of affordability without compromising on the neighborhood's prestige. Within four weeks, he received multiple inquiries and was able to negotiate with buyers eager to secure a deal in the area. John ultimately accepted an offer close to his asking price, successfully closing the sale within his desired timeframe.

Lesson Learned:

John's case demonstrates the effectiveness of anchor pricing in positioning a property as a value option in markets with diverse property values. By anchoring his price just below the higher-priced homes, John created an opportunity for buyers to see his home as an attractive alternative, allowing him to leverage the prestige of the neighborhood while appealing to budget-conscious buyers. This strategy is especially useful in areas with wide-ranging prices, as it allows sellers to position their homes competitively while benefiting from the market's overall high value perception.

Case Study 4:

Leveraging a Pricing Dashboard for Timely Adjustments

Overview:

Emma was selling her property in a neighborhood with fluctuating market conditions, where buyer interest and local sales trends could change rapidly. To stay competitive, Emma needed a proactive approach that would allow her to make informed pricing adjustments based on real-time data. Rather than setting a static price and waiting for offers, Emma created a pricing dashboard to monitor various market factors throughout her listing period.

Her dashboard tracked key metrics such as comparable sales, new listings, average days on market, buyer inquiries, and any local market news affecting property demand. With this dashboard, Emma could spot trends early, assess her property's competitiveness, and adjust her pricing as needed to stay aligned with market conditions.

Strategy and Execution:

1. Setting Up the Pricing Dashboard: Emma organized her dashboard with weekly updates on recent comparable sales, changes in local inventory, and average days on market for homes in her area. She created columns for data points such as listing prices, closing prices, property features, and price adjustments made by other sellers.

2. Monitoring Buyer Interest: Emma also tracked data on her own listing, including the number of inquiries, online views, and buyer feedback from showings. By recording this information weekly, she could gauge whether her listing was attracting the expected level of interest and compare it to similar properties.

3. Market Condition Tracking: Emma subscribed to a few local real estate news sources and tracked changes in interest rates, local economic conditions, and any new developments in her area. She updated her dashboard whenever a notable market change occurred, allowing her to see if these changes were impacting her property's appeal.

4. Data-Driven Price Adjustments: Emma set a strategy to review the dashboard every two weeks. If data suggested that similar properties were lowering prices or moving more quickly, she would consider a price adjustment. Emma's initial price was competitive, but after a few weeks of slower interest, her dashboard data showed that other listings were starting to lower

prices slightly. Based on this trend, Emma adjusted her price by 2% to maintain a competitive edge.

Outcome:

Emma's use of a pricing dashboard provided her with the insights she needed to make data-driven decisions. When her property initially saw limited interest, her dashboard revealed that other sellers were also adjusting prices. By following suit with a modest price reduction, she kept her listing competitive without significantly impacting her overall profit. This proactive approach helped Emma attract renewed interest, and within her target timeline, she received an offer that met her expectations. By closing the sale within her desired timeframe, she was able to avoid the risks of lingering on the market too long, such as price cuts or reduced buyer interest.

Lesson Learned:

Emma's experience demonstrates the value of a pricing dashboard in helping FSBO sellers respond effectively to market changes. By tracking real-time data, sellers can avoid the pitfalls of overpricing or underpricing in a fluctuating market. A dashboard not only provides a clear picture of how a listing is performing relative to similar properties but also empowers sellers to make timely adjustments that keep their property appealing. Emma's case illustrates that a proactive, data-driven approach can lead to a faster sale and a more satisfying outcome in dynamic real estate markets.

2. Avoiding Overpricing Pitfalls (Expanded)

Overpricing is a common issue that can lead to extended market time, price cuts, and reduced buyer interest. Here are some strategies for FSBO sellers to avoid these pitfalls.

Additional Overpricing Strategies

- Timing Adjustments Based on Market Feedback: If there's limited buyer interest after two weeks, sellers should consider reassessing the price. Reviewing other comparable listings can provide insight into whether adjustments are needed.
- Setting Milestones for Price Reviews: Establish specific timelines to reevaluate the price (e.g., at 15, 30, and 45 days) to keep the listing competitive and prevent the property from becoming stale.

Case Study 5:
Importance of Objectivity in Pricing

Overview:

Sam was selling his family home of over 30 years, a property filled with sentimental value and memories. Due to his personal attachment, Sam initially priced the home about 15% above the comparable market value, believing the unique history and emotional connection justified a premium. However, his emotional pricing led to limited interest and minimal buyer engagement during the first three months on the market. As he grew increasingly concerned about the lack of interest, Sam recognized the need to take a more objective, data-driven approach to pricing.

To realign his expectations, Sam conducted a thorough review of recent comparable sales in the area, carefully analyzing data on properties similar in size, age, and condition. He realized that his original price was well above what the market supported, even for a desirable property like his. By reassessing his property through an objective lens, Sam was able to make a more realistic pricing decision.

Strategy and Execution:

1. Confronting Emotional Bias: Initially, Sam's sentimental attachment clouded his judgment and influenced his percep-

tion of the home's value. Recognizing the issue, he decided to detach emotionally and consider the property's value strictly from a buyer's perspective.

2. Market Analysis and Price Comparison: Sam reviewed recent sales data for comparable properties, particularly focusing on those that had sold within the last 3-6 months. He analyzed factors such as price per square foot, condition, upgrades, and days on market for each comparable home. This data-driven approach helped him understand what buyers in his area were realistically willing to pay.

3. Price Adjustment Based on Objective Data: After evaluating the comps, Sam adjusted his asking price by lowering it to match the average market value for similar properties. This adjustment brought his price in line with buyer expectations and made it more competitive within the local market.

4. Enhanced Marketing with New Pricing: To refresh the listing and attract renewed interest, Sam also updated the property description to highlight recent improvements he had made. This strategy, combined with the new price, created a more compelling listing.

Outcome:

Within two weeks of adjusting the price, Sam received a competitive offer close to his new asking price. The data-driven adjustment not only attracted more attention but also helped him close the sale with terms that met his financial needs. By remaining objective, Sam was able to shift his focus from an emotionally charged valuation to a realistic one that aligned with market trends.

Lesson Learned:

Sam's experience highlights the importance of objectivity in pricing, especially when personal attachment is involved. Emotional connections can lead FSBO sellers to overestimate their property's value, which may deter buyers and prolong time on the market. Sam's case demonstrates that basing pricing decisions on objective data, such as recent comparable sales, ensures a competitive and market-aligned price. By taking an unbiased approach, FSBO sellers can avoid pricing pitfalls, attract more buyers, and ultimately achieve a successful sale.

Case Study 6:
Price Adjustment Based on Market Feedback

Overview:

Jake decided to list his home at a price slightly above comparable properties in his neighborhood, hoping to maximize his profit. Confident that the property's features and location would justify the premium, he set the price approximately 7% higher than recent sales in the area. However, after several weeks with minimal buyer interest and no offers, Jake realized his pricing strategy might be deterring potential buyers. Recognizing the need to adapt, Jake decided to review recent market data and analyze his listing performance based on market feedback.

Jake noticed that similar homes had recently sold after brief periods on the market and at more competitive prices. This realization prompted him to reduce his asking price, aiming to revitalize interest and stay competitive with other listings in his area.

Strategy and Execution:

1. Gathering Market Feedback: Jake monitored his listing metrics, including views, inquiries, and feedback from potential buyers. The low interest indicated that his initial price might not align with buyer expectations, signaling a need for adjustment.

2. Consulting Recent Data: Jake analyzed new comparable sales data to see how similar homes were performing. He noticed

that properties within a 5% lower price range were attracting significant buyer interest and selling more quickly. This insight helped him understand that his home's initial price was likely above market expectations.

3. Price Adjustment and Listing Refresh: Based on this data, Jake decided to reduce his price by 5%, bringing it more in line with comparable listings. He updated his online listing to reflect the new price and used the opportunity to refresh the photos and description to emphasize the property's key features.

4. Enhanced Marketing with New Price: Jake also highlighted the recent price reduction in the listing description and in his marketing efforts, noting that the property was now "priced to sell" to attract more attention. He strategically promoted the listing on social media and real estate platforms to reach a wider audience of potential buyers.

Outcome:

The price adjustment immediately generated renewed interest, with more inquiries coming in within days of the update. Shortly after the price reduction, Jake received a full-price offer from a motivated buyer who had been monitoring the property but initially found it overpriced. The timely price adjustment not only attracted more serious buyers but also helped Jake secure a sale close to his target price.

Lesson Learned:

Jake's experience highlights the value of responding quickly to market feedback and making strategic price adjustments when necessary. A timely reduction can help revitalize a listing, attract serious buyers, and prevent the property from lingering on the market. By staying attuned to buyer interest and adjusting based on data, FSBO sellers can keep their listings competitive and maintain momentum in the sales process.

4. Additional Tools and Resources for Pricing

Pricing Worksheets and Forms

- Pricing Strategy Checklist: A printable checklist to guide sellers through pricing steps, from setting a baseline to making timely adjustments.
- Offer Analysis Worksheet: This worksheet helps sellers compare offers objectively, weighing each based on price, contingencies, and terms for an informed decision.

Online Resources for Regular Market Monitoring

- Real Estate Market Analytics Platforms: Platforms like Realtor.com, CoreLogic, and local real estate databases provide valuable insights into trends and pricing strategies.
- Local Real Estate News Sites: Regularly monitoring real estate news or subscribing to local property market updates helps FSBO sellers stay aware of changes impacting demand and pricing.

5. FAQs and Common Questions About Pricing

This FAQ section addresses common pricing scenarios FSBO sellers face, offering guidance on how to navigate different situations effectively.

1. What if I don't receive any offers in the first few weeks?

- Answer: Consider refreshing the listing with updated photos or a new description, reassessing the price, and comparing it to recent sales of similar properties. This may attract renewed interest from buyers.

2. How do I handle low-ball offers?

- Answer: Develop a counteroffer strategy based on your minimum acceptable price. Use data from comparable sales to justify your counteroffer, which can lead to fair and productive negotiations.

3. What are the benefits of starting at a lower price point?

- Answer: Starting with a competitive price can attract more buyers and potentially lead to multiple offers, which may drive up the final sale price. A lower entry point often garners faster interest and reduces time on the market.

4. When should I consider a price reduction?

- Answer: Set a timeframe (e.g., every 30 days) to review the market response and adjust the price if necessary. Regularly reassessing the price helps keep the listing competitive and aligned with market trends.

5. What if my property sits on the market too long?

- Answer: If your property hasn't sold after an extended period, it might be perceived as overpriced. Try refreshing your marketing strategy or lowering the price slightly to reignite buyer interest.

6. How can I determine if my home is priced too high?

- Answer: Compare your listing to similar, recently sold properties. If comparable homes are selling faster at lower prices, it could indicate that your property is overpriced. Reviewing feedback from potential buyers can also provide insights.

7. Is it okay to price my home slightly above market value?

- Answer: While it's possible, pricing too high can lead to extended time on the market and fewer offers. If you're set on a higher price, be prepared to adjust quickly based on buyer response.

8. How do I use buyer feedback to adjust my price?

- Answer: If multiple buyers comment on the price or compare it unfavorably with other listings, consider this feedback when making price adjustments. Objective buyer feedback is valuable for understanding how your property compares to competing listings.

9. What if the market changes while my property is listed?

- Answer: Keep an eye on local trends and similar listings. If there's a sudden shift (e.g., increased inventory or interest rate changes), adjust your price to stay competitive within the current market conditions.

10. How can I justify my asking price to buyers?

- Answer: Provide data from a Comparative Market Analysis (CMA), showing comparable sales, property improvements, and unique features that support your price. Transparency with potential buyers can foster trust and confidence in your listing.

11. Should I adjust the price if the property doesn't appraise at the asking price?

- Answer: Yes, if an appraisal comes in lower than expected, consider lowering the price or negotiating with the buyer. Many buyers depend on the appraisal for financing, so adjusting the price may help keep the sale on track.

12. Can I start with a higher price and lower it later?

- Answer: This approach is common but can deter initial buyer interest. Many buyers prioritize newly listed properties, so setting a competitive price from the start often leads to a quicker sale. If you do start higher, monitor buyer interest closely and be ready to adjust.

13. How much should I lower the price if I need to adjust?

- Answer: Small reductions (e.g., 1-2%) may not significantly impact buyer interest, whereas a more noticeable adjustment (5-10%) can signal that you're serious about selling. The adjustment amount should be based on comparable sales and recent buyer feedback.

14. What's the risk of overpricing my property in a hot market?

- Answer: Even in a strong market, overpricing can cause your listing to stagnate. Buyers may still perceive your property as overpriced compared to similar homes, which can lead to extended time on the market and potential price cuts later on.

15. How can I attract more buyers without lowering my price?

- Answer: Enhance the listing's appeal with updated photos, a virtual tour, or a refreshed description highlighting unique features. Invest in targeted online ads or a flat-fee MLS listing to increase visibility. Small investments in staging or curb appeal can also improve buyer interest without a price reduction.

16. What if a buyer offers more than my asking price?

- Answer: Consider any contingencies in the offer, as well as the buyer's financial qualifications. Multiple offers may give you the opportunity to negotiate favorable terms, but ensure that the buyer's financing aligns with the offered price to avoid complications during appraisal.

17. How often should I review my pricing strategy?

- Answer: Set milestones to review your pricing every 15-30 days. During each review, assess recent sales, buyer feedback, and any market changes to determine if an adjustment is warranted.

Conclusion and Summary

A balanced, data-driven pricing approach is crucial for FSBO sellers to succeed in today's real estate market. Setting the right price from the beginning can mean the difference between a quick sale and a prolonged listing, ultimately impacting both profitability and market perception. This chapter has outlined the essential components of an effective pricing strategy, from understanding local trends and utilizing advanced pricing tools to avoiding common pitfalls and responding promptly to market feedback.

By leveraging resources such as pricing dashboards, market analytics, and Comparative Market Analyses (CMAs), FSBO sellers gain insights that allow them to make well-informed, competitive pricing decisions. The importance of objectivity in pricing cannot be overstated—by grounding their decisions in data rather than sentiment, sellers ensure their listings remain aligned with buyer expectations. The use of real-world case studies further illustrates how strategic adjustments, like anchor pricing or timely reductions, can drive buyer interest and result in favorable sale outcomes.

In addition to setting the right price, this chapter underscores the importance of ongoing review and adaptability. Markets can shift unexpectedly, and FSBO sellers benefit from establishing a system for regular review and adjustment of their pricing strategy. Proactively monitoring trends, engaging with buyer feedback, and making incremental adjustments help sellers avoid the risks of overpricing or underpricing in fluctuating conditions.

To summarize, effective pricing in FSBO sales is a combination of science and strategy. By applying market insights, utilizing pricing tools, and remaining flexible, sellers can achieve a successful sale while maximizing profitability. Equipped with a comprehensive pricing foundation, FSBO sellers are now empowered to approach the pricing process confidently, setting the stage for a successful sale that aligns with both their financial goals and market conditions. This chapter's guidance serves as a roadmap for navigating pricing with precision, ensuring FSBO sellers are well-prepared to make informed, proactive decisions throughout their selling journey.

References

CoreLogic. (2023). U.S. real estate market trends and data insights. CoreLogic. Retrieved from https://www.corelogic.com/

National Association of Realtors. (2023). 2023 profile of home buyers and sellers. National Association of Realtors. Retrieved from https://www.nar.realtor/research-and-statistics

Redfin Insights. (2023). Pricing strategies and market trends for home sellers. Redfin. Retrieved from https://www.redfin.com/news

Realtor.com. (2023). Understanding comparative market analysis for home pricing. Realtor.com. Retrieved from https://www.realtor.com/research/

Real Estate Marketing Insights. (2023). Real estate pricing tactics for competitive markets. Real Estate Marketing Insights. Retrieved from https://www.realestatemarketinginsights.com

Zillow Research. (2023). Strategies for effective home pricing and market analysis. Zillow Research. Retrieved from https://www.zillow.com/research

CHAPTER 4
LEGAL AND FINANCIAL ASPECTS OF FSBO

Selling a home independently requires a solid understanding of the legal and financial obligations involved in a real estate transaction. FSBO sellers must navigate contracts, manage documentation, and work through the closing process. While selling FSBO can save on commission fees, we highly recommend consulting a real estate attorney throughout the process to ensure compliance and avoid costly mistakes. Legal professionals can assist in interpreting and drafting documents, making sure all contracts meet local regulations, and protecting your interests at every step.

1. Key Contracts And Documentation

Proper documentation is critical in FSBO transactions. Each document must be completed accurately and comply with state laws to avoid delays, potential disputes, or even legal liabilities. Here are the essential documents FSBO sellers should prepare and understand:

1. **Purchase Agreement (Sales Contract)**
   - Purpose: The core agreement between buyer and seller, outlining the sale price, terms, contingencies, and conditions of the sale. This contract establishes the binding terms both parties agree to in the transaction.
   - Components: Include purchase price, earnest money deposit, contingencies (e.g., inspection, financing), closing date, and any additional terms.

- Recommendation: An attorney should review the purchase agreement before signing to ensure it includes essential clauses that protect the seller's interests and that no crucial terms are missing.

2. **Property Disclosure Forms**

- Purpose: Required in most states, this form details any known issues with the property (e.g., structural issues, environmental hazards, previous repairs). Disclosures protect both the buyer and the seller by ensuring full transparency.
- Types of Disclosures: Include information about the property's condition, environmental risks (like flood zones), and any material defects.
- Recommendation: Consult an attorney to ensure the disclosure complies with state laws, as failure to disclose issues can lead to legal liability.

3. **Title Report and Deed**

- Purpose: Confirms the property's legal ownership and any existing liens, claims, or restrictions that must be resolved before the sale.
- Deed Transfer: At closing, the deed transfers ownership from the seller to the buyer. This requires precise completion to ensure legality and validity.
- Recommendation: Work with an attorney and a title company to verify a clean title and to draft the deed transfer documentation accurately.

4. **Closing Statement (Settlement Statement)**

- Purpose: Summarizes all financial details of the transaction, including purchase price, prorated taxes, closing costs, and any credits. Ensures both buyer and seller understand their financial responsibilities.

- Recommendation: Have this document prepared by a title company or attorney to avoid errors and ensure full transparency.

5. **Other Contracts and Forms**

- Examples: Home inspection reports, lead-based paint disclosure (for homes built before 1978), homeowners' association (HOA) documents (if applicable), and loan payoff information (if a mortgage exists).
- Recommendation: Consult with an attorney to verify which forms are legally required in your state and ensure all are completed correctly.

2. Navigating The Closing Process

The closing process is the final step in selling a property FSBO, and it involves several critical actions to transfer ownership legally and financially. Here's an overview of the typical closing steps and responsibilities for FSBO sellers:

1. **Escrow Account Management**

- Purpose: Many transactions use an escrow account managed by a third-party title company or escrow service. This account holds the buyer's earnest money deposit, which is applied to the sale at closing.
- Action: Coordinate with a title company or attorney to set up the escrow account and manage the funds securely.

2. **Title Search and Insurance**

- Title Search: A title company performs a title search to verify that the property is free from liens, unpaid taxes, or ownership claims.

- Title Insurance: Protects both buyer and seller from potential title disputes after the sale. Title insurance is typically required by lenders but recommended even for cash transactions.
- Recommendation: Title insurance and a thorough title search are essential for a clean and smooth closing. Have an attorney review any title discrepancies that arise.

3. Preparing for the Final Walkthrough

- Purpose: The buyer conducts a walkthrough before closing to confirm that the property is in agreed-upon condition and that any negotiated repairs are complete.
- Seller's Role: Ensure the property is ready and repairs are complete as agreed upon in the purchase agreement. Address any last-minute issues promptly.

4. Reviewing and Signing Closing Documents

- Documents to Sign: This includes the deed, closing statement, title transfer forms, and any affidavits or disclosures required by state law.
- Recommendation: Since these documents are legally binding, consult an attorney to review each before signing. This will ensure the seller's interests are protected and prevent potential post-sale disputes.

5. Funds Transfer and Final Settlement

- Purpose: At closing, funds from the buyer (and lender, if applicable) are disbursed to the seller, and the deed is recorded with the local government to finalize the ownership transfer.
- Action: Confirm with the title company that all funds and settlement costs are accurate. Keep copies of all documents for future reference.

3. When To Consult A Real Estate Attorney

Even with careful preparation, FSBO transactions can be legally complex. A real estate attorney provides essential guidance, ensuring compliance with local laws, protecting the seller's interests, and avoiding potential issues. Here's when to consult an attorney:

1. Initial Contract Review and Negotiation

- Before entering into a binding agreement with the buyer, an attorney should review the purchase agreement to ensure it includes all necessary terms and protects the seller from liabilities.

2. Title and Disclosure Requirements

- Different states have unique requirements for property disclosures and title documentation. An attorney can confirm that these documents comply with state-specific laws and that no crucial information is omitted.

3. Resolving Disputes and Contingencies

- If contingencies arise (such as financing, inspection issues, or buyer demands), an attorney can help negotiate a solution, keeping the transaction on track while minimizing risks for the seller.

4. Closing Document Review

- The closing is a significant, legally binding event. An attorney should review all documents to verify accuracy and to ensure no terms could lead to post-sale disputes.

5. Handling Unexpected Issues

- In cases of unexpected challenges—such as title defects, liens, or buyer financing issues—having legal support is invaluable.

An attorney can guide the seller through resolution processes efficiently, protecting the seller's position.

CASE STUDY 1:

Importance of Accurate Property Disclosures

Overview

Megan, an FSBO seller, was preparing her property for sale and wanted to ensure full transparency regarding its condition. Her home had a history of minor water damage in the basement, which she had professionally repaired years earlier. Megan knew that disclosing this history was crucial to protect herself legally and avoid potential issues with buyers down the line.

Strategy and Execution

- **Creating a Disclosure Document**: Megan documented the history of water damage, the steps taken to repair it, and attached receipts from the repair company to confirm the work done.
- **Legal Consultation**: Unsure of the full disclosure requirements, Megan consulted a real estate attorney who reviewed her disclosure form to ensure it complied with state laws.
- **Pre-Sale Inspection**: To demonstrate the property's sound condition, Megan obtained a pre-sale inspection, which she included with the disclosure documents.

Outcome

Megan's transparency and thorough documentation reassured potential buyers, and the buyer ultimately waived further inspection after reviewing her disclosure and inspection report. The sale closed smoothly, and Megan avoided post-sale disputes related to property condition.

Lesson Learned

Accurate and complete property disclosures protect the seller from legal liabilities and help build trust with buyers. Consulting an attorney for disclosure requirements ensures compliance with state regulations, avoiding potential legal issues after the sale.

Case Study 2: Navigating Title Issues Before Closing

Overview

David was selling his home FSBO when a title search revealed an outstanding lien on the property. Although he was unaware of this lien, it posed a problem that needed resolution before the sale could proceed.

Strategy and Execution

- **Consulting a Real Estate Attorney**: David quickly engaged a real estate attorney to investigate the lien and determine its validity.
- **Negotiating with the Creditor**: His attorney worked with the creditor to verify the debt and arranged for a reduced payoff amount, saving David both time and money.
- **Clearing the Title**: Once the lien was resolved, David's attorney coordinated with the title company to update the title and provide the buyer with a clear title.

Outcome

David was able to close the sale on schedule thanks to his attorney's expertise. The attorney's proactive approach ensured the lien was handled correctly, preventing last-minute delays or the potential for legal issues after the sale.

Lesson Learned

FSBO sellers should obtain a title search early in the process to identify any title issues. When complications arise, a real estate attorney can efficiently resolve them, ensuring the sale proceeds smoothly and on time.

Case Study 3: Managing the Closing Process Independently

Overview

Jenna chose to sell her property without an agent and was determined to manage the closing process herself to save on costs. Although she felt confident about the steps involved, she knew she'd need some professional guidance to navigate the legal documents accurately.

Strategy and Execution

- **Hiring a Title Company**: Jenna hired a title company to handle escrow and title transfer and ensure all financial and legal requirements were met at closing.
- **Consulting an Attorney for Document Review**: Before closing, Jenna's attorney reviewed all documents, including the deed, settlement statement, and buyer contingencies, to confirm that they were accurate and protected her interests.
- **Preparing for the Closing Meeting**: Jenna organized all required documents, such as disclosure forms, inspection reports, and HOA documents, and worked with the attorney to clarify any points before finalizing the sale.

Outcome

Jenna successfully closed the sale on time, with the title company managing the escrow and her attorney providing guidance. She saved on agent fees while ensuring all legal aspects were properly handled, gaining confidence in the FSBO process.

Lesson Learned

The closing process can be managed independently, but working with a title company and consulting an attorney for document review provides essential support, ensuring the transaction is legally sound.

Case Study 4: Avoiding Post-Sale Legal Issues Through Clear Contracts

Overview

Mark, an FSBO seller, received an offer with several contingencies, including an inspection contingency and a clause allowing the buyer to cancel based on financing approval. Recognizing the potential for complications, Mark wanted to clarify these terms and protect himself from the risk of last-minute changes.

Strategy and Execution

- Drafting a Clear Purchase Agreement: Mark consulted an attorney to help draft a detailed purchase agreement that addressed each contingency in clear terms. The agreement specified deadlines for each contingency and outlined conditions under which the deposit could be retained.
- Contingency Management: The attorney helped Mark add language that required the buyer to complete the inspection and confirm financing within set timeframes, ensuring Mark could re-list the property promptly if needed.
- Closing Document Preparation: The attorney also prepared closing documents, ensuring each term was documented in accordance with the agreement.

Outcome

Mark's clear contract minimized ambiguity and provided a timeline for contingencies. The buyer's financing was approved on time, and the sale closed smoothly, with all parties meeting their obligations as outlined in the agreement.

Lesson Learned

Well-drafted contracts with specific terms for contingencies help FSBO sellers avoid legal issues, misunderstandings, and delays. An attorney's guidance is invaluable in crafting an agreement that protects the seller's interests and sets clear expectations for all parties.

Common Real Estate forms required by many and most states

There are several common real estate forms required in nearly every U.S. state for property sales. Although specific details and requirements can vary by state, the following forms are generally necessary for sellers to complete or provide:

1. Property Disclosure Form

- **Purpose**: This form requires sellers to disclose any known issues with the property, such as structural problems, past water damage, mold, lead paint, or pest infestations. The intent is to provide buyers with transparent information about the property's condition.
- **Variations**: While most states require a general disclosure form, some have specific forms (e.g., lead-based paint disclosure for homes built before 1978). Sellers should check their state's specific requirements, as some disclosures are legally mandated.

2. Lead-Based Paint Disclosure Form

- **Purpose**: Federal law requires this form for homes built before 1978 to inform buyers about potential lead-based paint hazards.
- **Details**: Sellers must disclose any known information about lead-based paint on the property, provide records or reports

(if available), and give buyers an EPA pamphlet on lead-based paint hazards.

3. Sales Contract (Purchase Agreement)

- **Purpose**: This legally binding contract outlines the terms of the sale, including the sale price, closing date, contingencies (e.g., inspection, financing), and other conditions agreed upon by the buyer and seller.
- **Details**: The purchase agreement is essential for any property sale and must meet state-specific guidelines. Many states provide standard purchase agreement forms, but it's wise to have an attorney review this contract to ensure compliance and protect both parties' interests.

4. Deed of Sale (or Warranty Deed/Quitclaim Deed)

- **Purpose**: The deed transfers ownership from the seller to the buyer. It is signed at closing and recorded with the local county clerk or recorder's office.
- **Details**: The specific type of deed varies; a warranty deed provides assurances to the buyer about the title, while a quitclaim deed transfers only the seller's interest without guarantees. States have unique requirements for deed language and recording.

5. Title Report (and Title Insurance)

- **Purpose**: A title report confirms the seller's legal ownership of the property and identifies any liens or encumbrances. Title insurance is usually recommended (or required) to protect both buyer and seller from title-related issues.
- **Details**: The title report is essential in clearing the title for transfer. Sellers must address any liens or claims that could affect the sale.

6. Settlement Statement (HUD-1 or Closing Disclosure)

- **Purpose:** This statement provides an itemized list of final costs associated with the sale, such as closing fees, title insurance, and escrow funds. It details each party's financial obligations and is reviewed before closing.
- **Details:** For most residential sales, this is now known as the "Closing Disclosure," which is required for buyers to review at least three days before closing. The HUD-1 is primarily used in cash sales and specific types of loans.

7. Bill of Sale (for Personal Property Included in Sale)

- **Purpose:** If the seller is including personal property with the sale (e.g., appliances, furniture), a bill of sale may be used to document this transfer.
- **Details:** Although not legally required in every transaction, a bill of sale can clarify what personal items are included and prevent misunderstandings.

8. Closing Affidavit (or Seller's Affidavit)

- **Purpose:** This form certifies that the seller has disclosed all material facts about the property and affirms that there are no undisclosed liens or issues that could affect the title.
- **Details:** Often signed at closing, this document assures the buyer and title company that no new issues have arisen since the title search.

9. Property Tax Documentation

- **Purpose:** Sellers provide evidence of paid property taxes and, in some cases, a proration of taxes up to the closing date.
- **Details:** States require proof that taxes are up-to-date, as unpaid taxes can complicate the title transfer.

10. Mortgage Payoff Statement (if applicable)

- **Purpose**: If the seller has an existing mortgage, this statement shows the remaining balance and any fees due upon payoff.
- **Details**: Mortgage lenders provide this document to ensure the loan is fully paid before transferring ownership, and it is typically settled at closing.

It's essential for FSBO sellers to work with a real estate attorney or title company to ensure compliance with state laws and to verify that all necessary forms are completed correctly.

Conclusion and Summary

Selling a home FSBO is an intricate process requiring attention to legal and financial details. While sellers can manage many steps independently, the involvement of a real estate attorney is highly recommended to protect their interests and ensure all transactions comply with state laws. From drafting the purchase agreement to closing document review, legal consultation minimizes risks, ensures compliance, and provides peace of mind throughout the sale process.

This chapter has outlined the key documents required in an FSBO transaction, the closing steps necessary to transfer ownership successfully, and the pivotal role of legal counsel. By staying informed and working closely with an attorney, FSBO sellers can confidently navigate the complexities of their sale, ensuring a legally sound and financireally rewarding outcome.

CHAPTER 5
MARKETING YOUR PROPERTY FOR MAXIMUM EXPOSURE

Marketing is one of the most critical steps in a FSBO (For Sale By Owner) sale. Effective marketing can lead to faster offers, stronger buyer interest, and even higher sale prices. This chapter covers essential components of a successful marketing plan, from creating a compelling listing to leveraging both digital and traditional marketing techniques. Real-world case studies illustrate how strategic marketing choices can maximize exposure and improve sale outcomes.

1. Creating A Compelling Listing

The listing serves as the first impression buyers will have of the property, making it essential to present it in the most attractive and accurate way possible.

Key Elements of a Strong Listing

- Professional Photography: Quality images can make or break a listing. Clear, high-resolution photos showing well-lit rooms, curb appeal, and key features (kitchen, bathrooms, living spaces) attract more interest. Many buyers are visual, and appealing photos can set a property apart.
- Descriptive Language: Use engaging language to highlight unique features, such as "spacious backyard oasis" or "modern open-concept kitchen." Include details that differentiate the property, like recent upgrades, proximity to local amenities, or neighborhood features.

- Key Information: Ensure the listing includes all essential details: square footage, number of bedrooms and bathrooms, age of the property, lot size, and any recent renovations or upgrades.
- Highlighting Unique Selling Points: Emphasize aspects that make the property appealing to specific buyer demographics (e.g., first-time buyers, growing families, retirees) or the local area (e.g., proximity to good schools, parks, or urban conveniences).

Tips for Crafting Effective Listing Descriptions

1. Focus on Benefits, Not Just Features: Describe how specific features will enhance the buyer's lifestyle (e.g., "enjoy morning coffee on the sunlit balcony").
2. Avoid Jargon: Use clear, accessible language that potential buyers can easily understand.
3. Stay Accurate: Transparency builds trust; avoid exaggerations or ambiguous claims that could mislead buyers.

2. Digital Marketing Strategies

With the majority of home buyers starting their search online, digital marketing is indispensable for FSBO sellers. Strategic use of online platforms can increase a listing's visibility and attract a larger pool of potential buyers.

Online Listing Platforms

- Zillow, Redfin, Realtor.com: These platforms are popular with buyers and allow FSBO sellers to reach a large audience.
- Flat-Fee MLS Listings: An MLS listing gives your property exposure across multiple sites, providing greater visibility without a traditional agent.

Social Media Marketing

- Facebook Marketplace: Ideal for local exposure, Facebook Marketplace allows sellers to reach an audience in their immediate area.
- Instagram: Visually driven, Instagram is a great platform for sharing high-quality photos and virtual tours. Using relevant hashtags (e.g., #dreamhome, #FSBO, #realestate) helps broaden reach.
- YouTube and Virtual Tours: Short video tours or walkthroughs can attract interest and make it easier for potential buyers to envision the space.

Paid Digital Advertising

- Google Ads and Facebook Ads: Targeted ads on Google and Facebook can drive traffic to the listing and increase exposure among relevant audiences. These ads allow sellers to set parameters like location, age group, and income level, ensuring the listing reaches those most likely to be interested.

Email Marketing

- Local Real Estate Newsletters: Collaborating with local newsletters or email lists can attract buyers looking in a specific neighborhood.
- Personal Network Outreach: Sellers can also reach out to friends, family, and colleagues via email, expanding their network of potential buyers through word of mouth.

3. Traditional Marketing Techniques

While digital marketing is highly effective, traditional methods are still valuable for reaching local buyers, especially those not actively browsing online listings.

Yard Signs and Directional Signs

- FSBO Yard Signs: A simple, effective way to attract local interest. Signs should include the property address, contact number, and an indication it's a FSBO listing.
- Directional Signs: Placing signs at key intersections helps guide local traffic toward the property, especially useful for open houses.

Open Houses and Property Showings

- Hosting Open Houses: Open houses provide an opportunity for buyers to tour the property and ask questions in person. Advertise open houses through local community boards, social media, and online platforms to maximize attendance.
- Appointment-Based Showings: For sellers preferring private viewings, scheduled showings offer more control and allow for a personalized walkthrough of the property.

Print Advertising

- Local Newspapers and Community Bulletins: Advertising in local print media can attract older buyers or those who prefer traditional media.
- Flyers and Brochures: Distributing professionally designed flyers at community centers, coffee shops, and local events can increase exposure to prospective buyers who might not be searching online.

Networking with Local Agents

- Agent Open Houses: Even if FSBO, inviting local agents for a tour can increase exposure as agents may have clients interested in similar properties.
- Co-Op with Buyer's Agents: FSBO sellers can offer a commission to buyer's agents, encouraging agents to bring clients and creating a win-win scenario.

CASE STUDIES

Case Study 1: Maximizing Exposure with Digital and Traditional Techniques

Overview

Sarah, a FSBO seller in a bustling suburban neighborhood, aimed to attract both local and out-of-town buyers to increase her chances of a fast sale. Understanding that a multi-faceted approach would reach a broader audience, she strategically used a combination of digital and traditional marketing methods. First, Sarah listed her home on high-traffic real estate websites like Zillow and Realtor.com, where potential buyers could easily view her listing. To capture local attention, she placed an eye-catching FSBO sign in her yard with her contact information, added directional signs at key intersections, and printed high-quality brochures that she left at local businesses, including coffee shops, community centers, and the library.

Additionally, Sarah created an Instagram account for her property, sharing photos, walkthroughs, and neighborhood highlights to appeal to local buyers and young families drawn to the area's amenities. She also posted a virtual tour video on YouTube, embedding the video link in her online listings, and ran a targeted Facebook ad campaign that focused on local users and out-of-state buyers relocating for work.

Strategy and Execution

- Professional Photography: Sarah hired a professional photographer to take high-quality photos of her home, capturing it in the best light and showcasing its features.
- Digital Listings on Major Platforms: By listing on Zillow and Realtor.com, she ensured that online buyers and those searching on mobile apps could easily access her property information.

- Social Media Campaigns: Sarah leveraged Instagram and Facebook, creating engaging posts and running a targeted ad campaign to capture interest from specific demographics, such as young families and professionals.
- Local Signage and Brochures: Eye-catching FSBO yard signs and strategic directional signs increased her property's visibility to local traffic. Brochures distributed at popular neighborhood spots expanded her local reach further.
- Virtual Tour on YouTube: A virtual tour on YouTube provided out-of-town buyers with a comprehensive look at the property, making it easier for them to envision the space.

Outcome

Sarah's multi-channel marketing strategy paid off. Within two weeks, she received several inquiries, including interest from local families and out-of-state buyers moving to the area. Ultimately, a buyer from the next town over made an offer, drawn in by the professional photography and FSBO signs that initially caught their attention while driving through the neighborhood. The blend of digital exposure and traditional, community-oriented marketing created a high level of visibility for her property, helping her secure a competitive offer sooner than expected.

Lesson Learned

This case demonstrates that combining digital and traditional marketing techniques broadens a property's reach, attracting both online and local buyers. Digital listings on popular platforms like Zillow and Realtor.com, coupled with engaging social media campaigns, can capture the attention of a tech-savvy audience, while yard signs, brochures, and local presence appeal to buyers within the community. By balancing these strategies, FSBO sellers can maximize exposure and accelerate the path to a successful sale, reaching a diverse group of potential buyers and increasing the likelihood of offers.

Case Study 2: Successful Marketing through Social Media and Virtual Tours

Overview

John, a FSBO seller in an urban area popular with younger buyers, recognized that social media would be the most effective way to reach his target audience. His goal was to showcase his home's modern layout and proximity to local amenities, aiming to appeal specifically to younger, tech-savvy buyers likely to search for properties on social platforms. John listed his home on Instagram and Facebook Marketplace and created a virtual tour video to provide a comprehensive view of the property for prospective buyers browsing online.

John created an Instagram profile exclusively for his home listing, sharing images, Stories, and Reels that featured different aspects of the home, such as the renovated kitchen, outdoor patio, and neighborhood views. To maximize visibility, he used popular real estate and neighborhood-specific hashtags. On Facebook, John posted the virtual tour video in local real estate groups and ran targeted ads aimed at users within a 25-mile radius, particularly those between the ages of 25 and 40. The ads also highlighted the property's key features and its proximity to amenities like public transportation, coffee shops, and parks, appealing directly to his ideal buyer profile.

Strategy and Execution

- Social Media Listings on Instagram and Facebook: By creating a presence on Instagram and Facebook Marketplace, John tapped into platforms frequently used by younger buyers. He leveraged Instagram Stories and Reels for engaging, interactive content, and posted the virtual tour on both platforms to offer an immersive viewing experience.
- Targeted Facebook Ads: Using Facebook Ads, John targeted users in his local area within his ideal age demographic. This

allowed him to reach a large number of local, likely buyers and increase awareness of the property in a short time.

- Professional Virtual Tour: John hired a videographer to create a virtual tour that walked viewers through the home, helping them visualize each room. This tour was linked to his Instagram bio, shared on Facebook groups, and embedded in his Marketplace listing to ensure maximum visibility.

- Community Engagement: John joined local online groups and forums, where he shared the listing and engaged with community members, answering questions and inviting them to check out the virtual tour.

Outcome

John's social media strategy attracted significant attention. Within a week, he received multiple inquiries from interested buyers, many of whom appreciated the convenience of being able to view the property remotely through the virtual tour. His targeted Facebook ads also generated substantial traffic, with serious buyers reaching out to schedule private showings after viewing the virtual tour. By the end of the month, John received a competitive offer from a buyer who first encountered the listing on Instagram and finalized the sale within his desired timeline.

Lesson Learned

This case highlights the effectiveness of social media marketing and virtual tours for engaging a tech-savvy audience, especially younger buyers. Platforms like Instagram and Facebook offer unique opportunities to present a property in creative ways that appeal to an online audience. Virtual tours provide an immersive experience that allows buyers to view a home from anywhere, while targeted ads ensure the property reaches a relevant local demographic. John's experience shows that a well-executed social media strategy can significantly boost visibility, generate buyer interest, and expedite the sales process, particularly in markets where tech-savvy buyers dominate.

Case Study 3: Attracting Out-of-Town Buyers with YouTube and Google Ads

Overview

Anne owned a property in a neighborhood known for attracting out-of-state buyers due to its proximity to prestigious universities and major corporate offices. Aware that many potential buyers were likely to be relocating from other states for work or academic purposes, Anne designed a targeted digital marketing strategy to reach buyers who couldn't attend local showings. She created a detailed video walkthrough of her home and posted it on YouTube to provide potential buyers with an immersive experience from a distance.

To expand her reach, Anne ran Google Ads targeting specific regions and demographics that aligned with her audience—primarily professionals relocating for work and families moving to be near universities. Her ads highlighted the home's spacious layout, proximity to reputable schools, and easy access to public transportation. She directed the ads to areas with large corporate offices and cities known for feeder schools to the nearby universities, aiming to appeal directly to those most likely to consider relocating.

Strategy and Execution

- YouTube Video Walkthrough: Anne worked with a videographer to create a high-quality video tour of her home, showcasing each room and outdoor spaces while emphasizing the property's unique features. She included a voiceover detailing each area's benefits, such as energy-efficient appliances, updated interiors, and scenic views.
- Google Ads Targeted to Relocation Hotspots: Using Google Ads, Anne targeted key out-of-state regions where many po-

tential buyers were based. Her ads emphasized keywords such as "relocation home near universities" and "family home near corporate offices," helping her connect with buyers searching specifically for homes in her area.

- SEO and Keywords for Broader Visibility: Anne optimized her YouTube video title, description, and tags with keywords like "relocation home," "near top universities," and "family-friendly neighborhood." This helped her video appear in relevant searches for out-of-town buyers looking for housing in her area.

- Local Connections for Out-of-State Buyers: Anne included links to community resources in her video description, such as nearby school profiles, local attractions, and corporate information, making it easy for buyers unfamiliar with the area to learn more about the neighborhood and amenities.

Outcome

Anne's strategy effectively attracted the attention of out-of-town buyers. Within the first week, her YouTube video had garnered significant views, with many viewers coming from regions where her Google Ads were targeted. Inquiries came in from several potential buyers who appreciated the detailed video walkthrough, as it provided them with a sense of the property's layout and condition without needing an in-person tour.

Three weeks after launching her Google Ads campaign, Anne received a competitive offer from a family relocating from another state due to a corporate transfer. The family, initially captivated by the YouTube video, felt confident making an offer without a physical tour after speaking with Anne and receiving additional information on the local area.

Lesson Learned

Anne's case illustrates the power of combining YouTube and targeted Google Ads to attract out-of-town buyers, especially in markets where relocation is common. Digital marketing with a focus on specific regions outside the local area can effectively expand reach and connect with buyers unable to tour in person. YouTube offers a flexible platform for detailed video walkthroughs, while Google Ads allow FSBO sellers to directly target regions and demographics likely to contain prospective buyers. This case demonstrates that strategic digital advertising, paired with engaging content, can open doors to a broader, geographically diverse buyer pool and accelerate the sale process.

Case Study 4: Creating Buzz with an Open House and Local Advertising

Overview

Maria owned a property in a close-knit suburban community where word-of-mouth and local visibility were essential for attracting potential buyers. She decided to hold an open house and strategically promoted it to maximize local attendance and generate buzz. Recognizing the importance of a strong local presence, Maria utilized a combination of community-focused advertising channels to spread the word and make her open house a memorable event.

To promote the event, she posted on popular local platforms, including community boards, neighborhood Facebook groups, and her homeowners association's online bulletin. Additionally, Maria created high-quality brochures featuring professional photos and property details to distribute at the open house, ensuring visitors had a tangible reminder of the property.

Strategy and Execution

- Targeted Community Advertising: Maria leveraged local community boards, neighborhood Facebook groups, and the online bulletin run by her homeowners association to reach her target audience directly. By focusing on hyper-local channels, she was able to attract community members who were familiar with the area or knew people looking to buy.

- Flyers and Signage: To increase foot traffic, Maria posted eye-catching flyers around local stores, coffee shops, and popular gathering spots. She also placed directional signs in high-traffic areas near the neighborhood on the day of the open house to guide passersby to the event.
- Creating an Inviting Open House Experience: Maria ensured that the open house felt welcoming by offering refreshments and arranging the home to highlight its best features. The kitchen and living room, which were the most attractive spaces, were staged with fresh flowers and natural lighting to create an appealing atmosphere.
- High-Quality Brochures for Follow-Up: To leave a lasting impression, Maria handed out professionally printed brochures that included high-resolution photos, details on the property's unique features, and her contact information. These brochures served as a visual reminder of the property and helped visitors easily recall the listing.

Outcome

The open house event attracted a strong turnout, with over 30 visitors attending. The neighborhood-focused advertising and the quality of the open house experience made a significant impact, as many attendees expressed immediate interest. Within days, Maria received two offers from prospective buyers who had attended the open house, leading to a successful sale shortly afterward.

Lesson Learned

Maria's case demonstrates the effectiveness of hosting a well-promoted open house in building excitement and generating interest in a local community. By advertising through community boards, social media, and local bulletins, Maria was able to maximize attendance, particularly from nearby residents who might have connections to potential buyers. The use of high-quality brochures helped ensure that the prop-

Marketing Your Property For Maximum Exposure

erty stayed top-of-mind after the event, reinforcing the property's appeal. This case shows that a thoughtfully planned and executed open house, combined with targeted local advertising, can attract serious buyers, create buzz, and expedite the path to receiving offers.

References for Chapter 5

Zillow Research. (2023). Effective online marketing strategies for FSBO sellers. *Zillow Research*. Retrieved from https://www.zillow.com/research

National Association of Realtors. (2023). Marketing trends in real estate: FSBO and beyond. *National Association of Realtors*. Retrieved from https://www.nar.realtor/research-and-statistics

Realtor.com. (2022). Using digital and traditional marketing for successful FSBO sales. *Realtor Insights*. Retrieved from https://www.realtor.com

Redfin Insights. (2022). Combining social media and traditional methods for home sales. *Redfin Insights*. Retrieved from https://www.redfin.com/news

CoreLogic. (2023). Maximizing property exposure through targeted advertising. *CoreLogic Market Trends*. Retrieved from https://www.corelogic.com

CHAPTER 6
MANAGING INQUIRIES, SHOWINGS, AND BUYER RELATIONSHIPS

In the FSBO process, managing inquiries, showings, and buyer relationships are crucial to building interest, establishing trust, and driving competitive offers. For FSBO sellers, navigating these interactions professionally and strategically can set the stage for a successful negotiation and sale.

1. Pre-Screening And Responding To Buyers

Effective pre-screening and timely responses play a critical role in identifying serious buyers and reducing time spent with casual or unqualified inquiries.

- Setting Pre-Screening Criteria: Establishing clear criteria can help sellers prioritize buyers with serious intent. Pre-screening can include questions about financing readiness, timeline, and preferred property features. These conversations can also help sellers avoid lengthy showings with buyers who may not align with the listing.

- Responding Promptly and Professionally: Quick responses create a strong first impression. Buyers often reach out to multiple listings, and a responsive, organized seller stands out. Use templates for common questions to save time while providing consistent, informative replies.

- Scheduling Showings with Efficiency in Mind: Using scheduling tools and organizing multiple showings in blocks can help sellers streamline the process, allowing them to present the property to several buyers within a short timeframe.

2. Negotiation Skills For Fsbo Sellers

Strong negotiation skills are essential in the FSBO sales process, as sellers must handle offers, counteroffers, and buyer requests independently.

- Setting Clear Boundaries and Goals: Before entering negotiations, sellers should define their lowest acceptable price, ideal closing date, and any concessions they're willing to make. This helps guide negotiations and ensures decisions align with their bottom line.
- Focusing on Win-Win Outcomes: Effective negotiators look for solutions that benefit both sides. Offering flexibility on minor terms, such as move-in dates or minor repairs, can encourage buyers to stay engaged and improve the likelihood of a successful agreement.
- Managing Counteroffers Strategically: When responding to offers, sellers should make counteroffers that reflect fair compromises. Sellers can use objective data, such as recent comps or appraisals, to justify their position, giving buyers confidence in the offer's fairness.

3. Building Trust and Positive Buyer Relationships

Creating a professional yet personable connection with potential buyers fosters trust and helps build momentum in the sale process.

- Being Transparent and Honest: Providing upfront information on the property's condition and any recent repairs or upgrades can reassure buyers and reduce the likelihood of complications later.

- Regular Follow-Up: Staying in touch with buyers after showings or open houses demonstrates engagement and can help keep the listing top-of-mind for interested buyers. A friendly follow-up email or message can prompt buyers to ask questions and possibly make an offer.
- Maintaining Flexibility with Showings: FSBO sellers should aim to be accommodating with showing schedules when possible. This flexibility can increase buyer satisfaction and encourage repeat visits, particularly for serious buyers considering multiple properties.

4. Handling Offers and Counteroffers

Accepting, rejecting, or countering offers effectively requires careful consideration and a structured approach.

- Evaluating Offers Objectively: Sellers should analyze each offer's financial components, including the purchase price, contingencies, and financing type. Comparing offers side-by-side helps sellers make informed choices.
- Making Calculated Counteroffers: Counteroffers are an opportunity to negotiate toward the seller's ideal terms. Sellers should carefully craft counteroffers to balance their goals with buyer expectations and avoid excessive back-and-forth.
- Responding to Low Offers: While low offers may seem discouraging, responding with a professional counteroffer keeps the door open. A well-reasoned counter, supported by property data, may lead to a more favorable outcome.

CASE STUDIES

Case Study 1: Pre-Screening for Serious Buyers

Overview:

Amanda owned a two-bedroom condo in a highly desirable urban neighborhood known for its proximity to public transit, restaurants, and cultural attractions. Given the area's popularity, Amanda anticipated strong interest from buyers but wanted to avoid spending time on casual inquiries that wouldn't lead to serious offers. To streamline the process, Amanda decided to implement a pre-screening strategy. This approach involved asking potential buyers a few targeted questions about their **financing status and timeline before scheduling showings.**

Strategy and Execution:

1. **Setting Up Pre-Screening Questions:** Amanda developed a set of standard questions to gauge buyer readiness. These included:

- "Have you been pre-approved for a mortgage, and at what amount?"
- "What is your preferred timeline for purchasing and moving?"
- "Are there any specific amenities or features you're looking for?" Amanda included these questions in her responses to initial inquiries, letting buyers know that answering them would help streamline the showing process.

2. **Screening for Financing Readiness:** By asking upfront about mortgage pre-approval, Amanda could prioritize buyers who were financially prepared. This step helped Amanda identify individuals who had been pre-approved for mortgages close to her asking price, reducing time spent on showings for buyers who might struggle to secure financing.

3. **Prioritizing Based on Timeline:** Amanda wanted to sell the condo within the next few months to align with her own relocation plans. By asking about buyers' timelines, she could avoid scheduling showings for those not ready to move within her timeframe, focusing instead on buyers prepared to make offers quickly.

4. **Organizing Showings Efficiently:** With responses from her pre-screening questions, Amanda scheduled showings in blocks for pre-qualified buyers. This approach allowed her to efficiently showcase the property to multiple serious buyers within a few hours on weekends, maximizing interest while minimizing disruptions to her schedule.

Outcome:

The pre-screening process proved effective in helping Amanda focus on serious, financially prepared buyers. She received an offer within a month from a buyer who was pre-approved and aligned with her desired closing timeline. By focusing on well-qualified buyers, Amanda avoided spending unnecessary time on showings that wouldn't likely lead to offers, allowing her to use her time more efficiently.

Lesson Learned:

Pre-screening questions are a valuable tool for FSBO sellers, particularly in high-interest areas where buyer inquiries can be overwhelming. By focusing on financing readiness and timeline, Amanda was able to filter out casual interest and concentrate on serious buyers. Her experience shows that a strategic pre-screening approach helps save time, facilitates more productive showings, and increases the chances of securing an offer from a qualified buyer.

Case Study 2: Successful Negotiation through Flexibility and Data

Overview:

Tom was selling his three-bedroom home in a suburban neighborhood and had set a competitive asking price based on a thorough market analysis. After listing the property, he received an offer from a potential buyer that was notably lower than his asking price. Initially disappointed by the low offer, Tom decided to approach the negotiation process strategically rather than declining outright. His goal was to create a dialogue that might lead to a price agreement closer to his expectations.

Strategy and Execution:

1. Leveraging Sales Data: Instead of countering with an emotional response, Tom began by compiling recent sales data for similar properties in the area. He highlighted nearby homes with comparable features, condition, and size that had sold at or near his asking price within the past few months. This data helped Tom demonstrate his home's fair market value to the buyer.

2. Presenting a Data-Driven Counteroffer: Tom used the sales data as the basis for a counteroffer that was slightly below his initial asking price but still higher than the buyer's original offer. By sharing his findings, Tom was able to convey that his asking price was not arbitrary but aligned with the current market.

3. Offering Flexibility on Closing Timeline: To show his willingness to work with the buyer, Tom offered flexibility on the closing date. He recognized that the buyer needed additional time to finalize financing arrangements, so he proposed an extended closing timeline. This flexibility demonstrated Tom's desire to accommodate the buyer's needs, creating goodwill and a cooperative atmosphere.

4. Creating a Collaborative Negotiation: Rather than approaching the negotiation as a rigid back-and-forth, Tom focused on establishing a cooperative tone. He presented his counteroffer and flexibility as a way to find a solution that worked for both parties. This collaborative approach helped build rapport and encouraged the buyer to engage more openly in the negotiation.

Outcome:

The buyer responded positively to Tom's data-driven counteroffer and appreciated the flexibility on the closing timeline. Recognizing the property's fair market value, the buyer agreed to meet Tom halfway on the price. Within two weeks, they reached an agreement and finalized the sale, which allowed both parties to feel satisfied with the outcome.

Lesson Learned:

Tom's experience demonstrates that successful negotiation in FSBO sales can be achieved by combining objective data with a flexible approach. By backing up his counteroffer with concrete market data and showing a willingness to accommodate the buyer's timeline, Tom fostered a collaborative atmosphere that ultimately led to a mutually beneficial agreement. His case highlights the importance of balancing firmness with flexibility, allowing FSBO sellers to negotiate confidently while maintaining a positive relationship with potential buyers.

Case Study 3: Building Buyer Trust through Transparency

Overview:

Lisa was selling her single-family home, a charming property with a few minor issues, including a leaky faucet and some chipped paint on the exterior. Knowing these minor repairs might raise questions for potential buyers, she worried they could lead to prolonged negotiations or even deter some buyers altogether. To address this proactively, Lisa decided to be transparent about the home's condition in her listing.

Strategy and Execution:

1. Disclosing Repairs in the Listing: Lisa detailed the minor issues upfront in her listing description, explaining that while the home had been well-maintained, a few repairs were needed. This transparency provided buyers with a clear understanding

of what to expect before even visiting the property, reducing the likelihood of negative surprises.

2. Offering a Repair Credit: To further reassure buyers, Lisa offered a small credit to cover the estimated repair costs. This credit not only made the repairs a non-issue for prospective buyers but also showed her willingness to support a fair deal. The credit was positioned as an "as-is" sale bonus, which attracted buyers who appreciated the financial flexibility.

3. Emphasizing Transparency in Communications: When responding to buyer inquiries and during showings, Lisa continued her transparent approach. She openly discussed the repairs, provided estimates for the work, and explained why she was offering the credit. Her forthrightness created a sense of trust and made buyers feel comfortable with the condition of the property.

4. Highlighting the Positive Aspects: Lisa balanced her honesty about the minor issues with an emphasis on the home's strengths, such as a recently renovated kitchen and a spacious backyard. By presenting the home's condition holistically, she showed that while there were minor repairs, the property offered substantial value.

Outcome:

Lisa's transparency created a positive impression on potential buyers, with several expressing appreciation for her honesty. One buyer even commented on how her upfront approach made her seem trustworthy, which factored into their decision to make an offer. Within three weeks, Lisa received an offer close to her asking price from a buyer who appreciated her openness and the repair credit offered.

Lesson Learned:

Lisa's case illustrates that transparency about property conditions can significantly improve buyer trust, making them more likely to feel comfortable and engaged in the buying process. Disclosing issues upfront helps avoid surprises during inspections and creates a foundation of honesty, leading to smoother negotiations. Her experience shows that an honest approach can make FSBO sellers stand out and lead to a quicker, smoother sale, even if there are minor property issues to address.

Case Study 4: Leveraging Counteroffers to Reach a Win-Win

Overview:

Mark was selling his three-bedroom home in a competitive market but received an initial offer significantly below his asking price. Although he was initially disappointed, he decided to approach the offer as an opportunity to negotiate rather than reject it outright. Recognizing that a flexible negotiation could still result in a favorable outcome, Mark crafted a counteroffer aimed at bridging the price gap while maintaining his target goals.

Strategy and Execution:

1. Assessing Key Goals: Mark prioritized achieving a price closer to his asking amount, but he was willing to offer concessions on non-essential terms. He identified closing costs as an area where he could be flexible, recognizing that this might make his counteroffer more appealing to the buyer.
2. Creating a Strategic Counteroffer: Instead of countering solely on price, Mark crafted a counteroffer that was closer to his original asking price but included an agreement to cover a portion of the buyer's closing costs. This allowed him to maintain the home's perceived value while making the offer more attractive for the buyer by reducing their immediate financial burden.

3. Emphasizing the Benefits: In presenting the counteroffer, Mark highlighted the advantages to the buyer, such as a reduced out-of-pocket expense at closing. By framing the counteroffer as a collaborative solution, he aimed to create a sense of partnership with the buyer, helping them see the negotiation as mutually beneficial.

4. Maintaining Open Communication: Mark remained open to further negotiations, responding promptly to the buyer's questions and clarifying any details they had about the counteroffer. This transparent approach built rapport and demonstrated his willingness to work toward a fair agreement.

Outcome:

Mark's counteroffer strategy proved effective. The buyer appreciated the closing cost concession, which helped them overcome their initial hesitation regarding the higher price. Satisfied with the financial balance, they accepted Mark's counteroffer, and the sale proceeded smoothly to closing within a month.

Lesson Learned:

Mark's case highlights the value of strategic counteroffers that include concessions on minor terms, such as closing costs. By focusing on creating a win-win solution, FSBO sellers can bridge price gaps without compromising their key financial goals. This approach can help build goodwill, ease negotiations, and increase the likelihood of a successful sale. Mark's experience shows that flexibility on smaller terms can make a significant difference in meeting both parties' needs and facilitating a positive outcome.

Reference List for Chapter 6

National Association of Realtors. (2023). *FSBO Negotiation Tips for Sellers.* Retrieved from [NAR Website]

Zillow Research. (2023). *Best Practices for Handling Showings and Buyer*

Relationships. Retrieved from [Zillow Research]

Realtor.com. (2023). *How to Make Counteroffers as a FSBO Seller.* Retrieved from [Realtor.com]

FSBO Guide. (2023). *Managing Buyer Inquiries and Building Trust.* Retrieved from [FSBO Guide Website]

CHAPTER 7
POST-SALE CONSIDERATIONS

After completing the sale of a property, FSBO sellers must address several key steps to ensure a smooth transition, manage any financial impacts, and fulfill all legal requirements. This chapter covers essential post-sale considerations, from coordinating the move-out process and key handover to understanding the tax implications and potential capital gains from the sale.

1. Moving Out And Handover Of Keys

Once the sale is finalized, a seamless move-out and handover of the property are crucial to fulfilling the seller's obligations and leaving a positive impression on the buyer.

A. Planning the Move-Out Process

- **Set a Timeline**: Establish a clear timeline for moving out based on the closing date. FSBO sellers should coordinate their moving schedule to ensure they can vacate the property in time for the buyer's possession.
- **Hire Movers and Organize Packing**: Schedule movers or rent a truck, and organize the packing process well in advance. Decluttering beforehand can help streamline the move and leave the home in good condition.
- **Prepare for Cleaning and Repairs**: Many FSBO sellers choose to clean the property thoroughly before handover. Consider

minor repairs or touch-ups to ensure the home is presentable and meets the conditions agreed upon in the sale.

- **Disconnect Utilities and Forward Mail**: Schedule the disconnection of utilities like electricity, gas, and water to coincide with the closing date. Additionally, forward any mail to your new address to avoid disruptions.

B. Handover of Keys and Access Details

- **Prepare Key Copies**: Ensure the buyer receives all necessary keys, including those for doors, garage, storage areas, and any other secured spaces.
- **Documenting the Condition**: Take photographs or video of the home's condition on the day of handover, which may be useful if any disputes arise later.
- **Transfer of Property Documents**: If there are property documents, warranties, or appliance manuals that the buyer needs, provide these during the handover. Additionally, include information on local services or recommendations if relevant.
- **Final Walk-Through with Buyer**: If possible, a final walk-through with the buyer before closing can clarify any questions and finalize the handover in a friendly, organized manner.

2. Tax Implications And Capital Gains

Selling a property can have significant tax implications, particularly when it comes to capital gains tax. It's essential for FSBO sellers to understand the tax considerations involved and consult with a tax professional to ensure compliance.

A. Understanding Capital Gains Tax

- **What are Capital Gains?**: Capital gains refer to the profit made from the sale of a property that has appreciated in value. The IRS imposes capital gains tax on this profit if it exceeds certain exemption limits.

- **Primary Residence Exemption**: For many homeowners, the primary residence exemption can reduce or eliminate capital gains tax. If the property was the seller's primary residence for at least two of the five years preceding the sale, they may exclude up to $250,000 in capital gains ($500,000 for married couples).
- **Long-Term vs. Short-Term Gains**: Properties held for more than one year qualify for long-term capital gains tax rates, which are lower than short-term rates. Properties held for less than a year are subject to short-term capital gains tax, which is taxed at regular income rates.

B. Deductions and Adjustments to Capital Gains

- **Improvements and Selling Costs**: FSBO sellers may reduce their capital gains by deducting the cost of home improvements, renovations, and selling expenses (e.g., advertising, legal fees, and moving costs) from the final sale price. Accurate record-keeping of these expenses is crucial.
- **Depreciation Recapture**: For properties previously rented or used for business, depreciation claimed on the property may be subject to recapture, increasing the taxable capital gains.
- **State and Local Taxes**: Capital gains tax varies by state, and some states may impose additional taxes on the sale of property. Sellers should consult a tax professional to understand state-specific tax implications.

C. Documentation for Tax Purposes

- **Maintain Records of Sale and Expenses**: FSBO sellers should keep copies of the purchase agreement, closing statement, and receipts for any home improvements. These records will be essential when calculating capital gains and reporting the sale on tax returns.

- **Seek Professional Advice**: Consulting a tax professional can help sellers maximize exemptions, navigate deductions, and accurately report capital gains. A professional can also advise on timing the sale if there are potential tax advantages.

CASE STUDIES

Case Study 1: Smooth Move-Out and Key Handover

Overview:

Mike, a FSBO (For Sale By Owner) seller, recently sold his single-family home in a quiet suburban neighborhood. While preparing for the closing, he understood that his move-out and handover would be critical to leaving a positive impression on the buyer and ensuring a smooth transition. With the buyer's scheduled possession date approaching, Mike planned the move meticulously to align with the closing day, aiming to avoid last-minute stress or potential delays.

Planning and Execution:

1. **Coordinating the Move-Out:** Mike began by setting a clear timeline for packing and moving out, giving himself ample time to organize. He scheduled professional movers a week before the possession date to ensure he could vacate comfortably without any rush. During this time, Mike also managed to complete packing gradually, allowing him to focus on maintaining the property's cleanliness and good condition.

2. **Organizing Packing and Decluttering:** Mike took the opportunity to declutter and dispose of items that wouldn't be moving with him. By donating or recycling unneeded items, he was able to reduce his moving load and keep the home's appearance tidy for any last-minute visits by the buyer. This

also meant fewer packing supplies and a cleaner space for the buyer's first impression.

3. **Thorough Cleaning and Minor Repairs:** Understanding that a clean and well-maintained home would leave a lasting impact, Mike took the extra step to thoroughly clean the property. He hired a cleaning service for a deep clean, covering areas like carpets, windows, kitchen appliances, and bathrooms. Additionally, Mike addressed a few minor repairs, such as fixing a loose cabinet hinge and patching small nail holes from picture frames, to make the home move-in ready.

4. **Scheduling Utility Transfers and Mail Forwarding:** Mike scheduled the disconnection of utilities, such as electricity, water, and gas, to take effect on the day of closing. He also forwarded his mail to his new address a week in advance, which helped prevent any lost mail during the transition.

5. **Handover of Keys and Documentation:** On the day of closing, Mike met with the buyer to formally hand over all property keys, including those for the front door, garage, storage shed, and any other locked areas. He also provided the buyer with essential property documents, such as appliance manuals, warranty information, and a list of trusted local service providers for landscaping and plumbing needs. To document the property's final condition, Mike took photographs of each room before departing, which could serve as proof of the home's condition if any disputes arose later.

6. **Final Walk-Through with Buyer:** To ensure everything was satisfactory, Mike invited the buyer for a brief walk-through of the home before leaving. During the walk-through, he took time to answer any questions, share helpful maintenance tips, and even point out specific features like the seasonal irrigation system and smart home devices, leaving the buyer feeling informed and at ease.

Outcome:

Mike's well-coordinated move-out and organized handover process resulted in a positive experience for both him and the buyer. The buyer expressed gratitude for the property's pristine condition and appreciated Mike's attention to detail and helpfulness during the transition. By ensuring the home was spotless and by providing necessary documents, Mike created a smooth handover experience that left the buyer satisfied and confident in their new purchase.

Lesson Learned:

Mike's case highlights the importance of a well-planned move-out and property handover in a successful FSBO transaction. Taking steps to coordinate moving logistics, thoroughly cleaning the property, and providing key documentation can enhance the overall sale experience and foster positive rapport with the buyer. A smooth transition reflects positively on the seller and minimizes potential post-sale disputes, leaving both parties with a sense of closure and satisfaction.

Case Study 2: Reducing Capital Gains with Home Improvements

Overview:

Susan, a long-time homeowner, decided to sell her property after it had appreciated significantly in value over the years. While she was pleased with the substantial profit from the sale, she was also aware that her capital gains might be subject to tax, which could reduce her net proceeds. Knowing that there were ways to potentially lower her capital gains tax liability, Susan took the proactive step of reviewing all the home improvements and upgrades she had completed during her ownership. These included a kitchen remodel, bathroom updates, landscaping improvements, and other value-enhancing renovations.

Steps Taken:

1. **Gathering Documentation for Home Improvements:** Susan went through her records and gathered receipts, invoices, and any contractor agreements from her home improvement projects. She organized the documentation to ensure she had clear records of each project's cost, timeline, and nature of work, which was critical for substantiating her claims for tax purposes.

2. Consulting a Tax Advisor: Understanding the complexities of capital gains tax, Susan consulted with a tax professional who specialized in real estate transactions. Together, they reviewed her records and identified which home improvements qualified for deductions. The tax advisor explained that only improvements that added value to the property or extended its useful life could be deducted from the sale price to reduce her capital gains.

3. **Applying the Primary Residence Exemption:** Susan qualified for the primary residence exemption because she had lived in the home for at least two of the last five years prior to the sale. This exemption allowed her to exclude up to $250,000 of capital gains (or $500,000 if filing jointly with her spouse), significantly lowering her taxable gain.

4. **Calculating Adjusted Basis:** With the tax advisor's guidance, Susan calculated her adjusted basis in the home by adding the cost of qualifying improvements to her original purchase price. This adjusted basis represented her initial investment plus the value she added through improvements, reducing her overall gain for tax purposes. For example, the kitchen remodel, which cost $20,000, and the landscaping upgrades, totaling $5,000, were substantial additions that increased her adjusted basis and lowered her taxable gain.

- **Deducting Selling Expenses:** In addition to home improvements, Susan also deducted eligible selling expenses from her capital gains. These included advertising fees, legal fees, and any other closing costs directly associated with selling the property. By carefully itemizing and deducting these expenses, she further minimized her capital gains.

Outcome:

With careful planning and documentation, Susan successfully reduced her capital gains tax liability. Her tax advisor helped her optimize deductions by applying the primary residence exemption and factoring in the costs of qualified home improvements and selling expenses. As a result, her taxable gain was significantly lower, allowing her to retain more of the profit from the sale.

Lesson Learned:

Susan's experience underscores the financial benefits of tracking home improvement expenses and seeking professional tax advice when selling a property. By keeping detailed records of improvements and working with a tax expert, FSBO sellers can leverage deductions to minimize capital gains tax and maximize their profit. For homeowners who have invested in their property over time, these strategies are essential for a tax-efficient sale, ensuring that sellers benefit from the full potential of their investment.

Case Study 3: Primary Residence Exemption for Tax Savings

Overview:

James and Lisa, a married couple, decided to sell their primary residence in which they had lived for the past three years. Over those years, their property had appreciated significantly, and they were excited about the potential profit. However, they were also concerned about the impact of capital gains taxes on their proceeds. Aware of the IRS primary residence exemption, they decided to confirm their eligibility and understand how much of their gain could be excluded from taxes.

Steps Taken:

1. **Confirming Residency Requirements:** James and Lisa reviewed the primary residence exemption rules to confirm their eligibility. According to the IRS, to qualify, homeowners must have used the property as their main residence for at least two of the five years prior to the sale. Having lived in the home consistently for three years, they met the residency requirement comfortably.

2. **Understanding the Exemption Limits:** As a married couple filing jointly, James and Lisa learned they were eligible to exclude up to $500,000 in capital gains from the sale of their primary residence. For single filers, the limit is $250,000. This meant they could potentially avoid paying taxes on a significant portion of their profit, providing a substantial financial benefit.

3. **Calculating Capital Gains:** Working with a tax advisor, they calculated their capital gain by subtracting their adjusted basis in the home from the sale price. Their adjusted basis included the original purchase price plus qualifying home improvements they had made over the years. By accurately calculating this, they ensured that they maximized their exclusion amount without overestimating their taxable gain.

4. Applying the Exemption: With a clear understanding of their capital gain and eligibility, James and Lisa claimed the $500,000 exclusion on their tax return. The advisor helped them apply this exemption correctly, allowing them to exclude the full amount of their gain from taxable income. They

filed their taxes with confidence, knowing they had correctly claimed all available benefits under IRS rules.

5. **Filing with Documentation:** To avoid any issues with the IRS, James and Lisa kept comprehensive documentation, including their purchase agreement, records of home improvements, and proof of residency, such as utility bills and mail addressed to their home. This documentation provided evidence of both their investment in the property and their eligibility for the exemption.

Outcome:

By meeting the primary residence exemption criteria, James and Lisa were able to exclude their capital gain up to the $500,000 limit, saving them a substantial amount in taxes. This tax-saving strategy allowed them to retain the vast majority of their sale proceeds, enabling them to invest in their next home and secure their financial future. Their thorough preparation and adherence to IRS rules made the tax filing process smooth and worry-free.

Lesson Learned:

James and Lisa's experience illustrates the financial advantage of the primary residence exemption for FSBO sellers. The exemption provides a significant tax benefit, especially for long-term homeowners who have seen substantial appreciation in their property's value. Ensuring eligibility by meeting the IRS residency requirement is crucial for taking full advantage of this exclusion. Proper documentation and a clear understanding of tax rules can help FSBO sellers maximize their profit while minimizing their tax liability. This case demonstrates that careful planning and compliance with tax requirements can significantly enhance the financial outcome of a property sale.

Case Study 4: Impact of Short-Term Capital Gains on Profit

Overview:

Rachel owned an investment property that she had purchased nine months prior. With the property's value increasing unexpectedly due to a local housing boom, she decided to sell it and cash in on the appreciated value. However, because Rachel hadn't held the property for at least one year, her sale was subject to short-term capital gains tax, which is taxed at her ordinary income tax rate rather than the lower long-term capital gains rate. This tax implication significantly affected her overall profit.

Steps Taken:

1. **Property Purchase and Quick Resale Decision**: Rachel purchased the property intending to hold it long-term, but when the local market saw a spike in demand, she received several offers well above her purchase price. This opportunity to realize a profit led her to consider a quick sale, especially as she hadn't planned for such immediate appreciation.

2. **Consulting a Tax Professional**: Unsure of the tax implications, Rachel consulted a tax advisor to understand how her gain from the sale would be taxed. The advisor explained that, since she had owned the property for less than one year, her profit would be subject to short-term capital gains tax, which is taxed at her regular income tax rate. This rate was significantly higher than the long-term capital gains rate that applies to properties held for over a year.

3. **Calculating Short-Term Capital Gains**: The advisor helped Rachel calculate her taxable gain by taking the sale price, subtracting her initial purchase price, and deducting allowable expenses, such as closing costs and certain property-related improvements. The resulting gain, subject to short-term capital

gains tax, was substantial and reduced her anticipated profit considerably.

4. **Reviewing Alternative Strategies**: Rachel's tax advisor pointed out that if she had held the property for just three more months, her gain would have qualified for the lower long-term capital gains rate. By waiting, she could have significantly reduced her tax liability. They discussed the potential value of delaying the sale, but since the property was already under contract and she was eager to capitalize on the current market, she proceeded with the sale.

5. **Filing and Tax Impact**: When filing her taxes, Rachel paid the short-term capital gains tax rate on her profit, which was roughly 10-20% higher than the long-term rate she would have paid if she had held the property for at least a year. This reduced her net profit significantly, leaving her with a much smaller gain than anticipated.

Outcome:

The higher tax rate on Rachel's short-term gain had a substantial impact on her overall profit. She realized that by selling the property before reaching the one-year ownership mark, she had missed out on the more favorable long-term capital gains rate. This experience emphasized the importance of timing property sales in investment strategy, especially for investors looking to maximize after-tax returns.

Lesson Learned:

Rachel's experience highlights the value of holding investment properties for over a year to qualify for the lower long-term capital gains tax rate. By understanding the tax implications of short-term versus long-term capital gains, FSBO sellers and property investors can make more informed decisions on the timing of sales to maximize their net profit. For investment properties, carefully planning the holding period can lead to substantial tax savings and a better financial outcome.

This case underscores the importance of integrating tax strategies into real estate investment plans to enhance profitability.

References for Chapter 7

Internal Revenue Service (IRS). (2023). *Publication 523: Selling Your Home.* Retrieved from https://www.irs.gov/publications

National Association of Realtors (NAR). (2023). *Guide to Tax Implications in Real Estate Sales.* Retrieved from https://www.nar.realtor/tax

Homeowner's Guide to Capital Gains Tax. (2023). *Understanding Exemptions, Deductions, and Tax Benefits in Property Sales.* Real Estate Tax Journal, 15(2), 12–18.

American Institute of Certified Public Accountants (AICPA). (2022). *Tax Considerations for Real Estate Transactions.* Retrieved from https://www.aicpa.org/tax

Appendix A: FSBO Expense Tracking and Budget Form

Expense Category	Budgeted Cost	Actual Cost	Notes
Flat-Fee MLS Listing			MLS access to increase listing visibility
Professional Photography			Essential for high-quality online visuals
Videography/Virtual Tour			Virtual tours for enhanced buyer engagement
Staging			Professional staging to improve home appeal

Targeted Advertising			Online ads on platforms like Zillow, Facebook
Legal Consultation			Legal review of contracts and disclosures
Pre-Listing Appraisal			Optional appraisal to set a competitive price
Pre-Listing Inspection			Identify issues before listing the property
Miscellaneous Fees			Supplies, yard signs, and additional expenses

Total Budgeted Cost: _____

Total Actual Cost: _____

Appendix B: Comparative Market Analysis (CMA) Worksheet

Comparable Property	Sale Price	Square Footage	Bed-rooms	Bath-rooms	Price per Sq Ft	Adjust-ments (e.g., Up-grades, Condi-tion)	Adjusted Sale Price
Property 1							
Property 2							
Property 3							

Median Price per Sq Ft: _____							
Suggested List-ing Price Range: _____							

Instructions for Use:

1. **Identify Comparable Properties**: Find 2-3 recently sold properties in the area similar in size, features, and location.
2. **Input Data**: Fill in the sale price, square footage, bedrooms, bathrooms, and calculated price per square foot for each comparable property.
3. **Adjustments**: Note any adjustments needed to account for differences (e.g., if your property has a larger lot or recent upgrades).
4. **Determine Median Price and Suggested Listing Price Range**: Calculate the median price per square foot to help estimate your property's suggested price range based on the adjusted comps.

Appendix C: Marketing Strategy and Listing Preparation Checklist

Marketing Activity	Date Scheduled	Status	Notes/Links
MLS Listing Creation		Not Started	Flat-fee MLS provider link
Professional Photography Session		Not Started	Date of photoshoot, photographer contact information

Virtual Tour Creation		Not Started	Link to virtual tour service or videographer
Online Advertising		Not Started	Links to Zillow, Redfin, or local real estate websites
Social Media Promotions		Not Started	Facebook Marketplace, Instagram, or other platforms
Open House 1		Not Started	Date and time, RSVP details
Open House 2		Not Started	Date and time, RSVP details
Yard Sign Placement		Not Started	Location of yard sign and contact info on sign
Print Flyers/Property Brochures		Not Started	Include property details, contact info
Post on Local Online Forums/Groups		Not Started	Links to neighborhood or city-based online forums

Instructions for Use:

1. **Complete Each Marketing Activity**: Fill in the date and status for each activity as it's scheduled or completed.
2. **Add Notes/Links**: Use this section to add essential information, such as URLs to listings, contact details, or links to social media posts, for easy access.
3. **Monitor Status**: Track the progress by updating the "Status" column, moving from "Not Started" to "In Progress" and "Completed" as you proceed.

Appendix D: Property Disclosure Form

Property Address: _____

Seller's Name: _____

Date Completed: _____

1. Property Condition

Condition/Feature	Yes/No	Details/Description
Roof Condition Issues		
Foundation Issues		
Plumbing Issues		
Electrical Issues		
HVAC (Heating & Cooling)		
Water Damage/Leaks		
Mold or Mildew		
Termite or Pest Issues		
Other Structural Issues		

2. Environmental Concerns

Environmental Concern	Yes/No	Details/Description
Lead-Based Paint		
Flooding History		
Radon Presence		
Asbestos		

Hazardous Materials Nearby		
Noise Pollution (Traffic, etc.)		

3. Recent Repairs and Upgrades

Repair/Upgrade	Year Completed	Details/Description
Roof Replacement		
Foundation Repair		
Plumbing Update		
Electrical Upgrade		
Kitchen Renovation		
Bathroom Renovation		
HVAC Replacement		
Landscaping Improvements		

4. Neighborhood and Property-Related Disclosures

Concern	Yes/No	Details/Description
Nearby Construction Projects		
Planned Zoning Changes		
Noise from Traffic/Railroad		
Odors or Pollution		

Seller's Acknowledgment: By signing below, I/we affirm that the information provided is accurate to the best of my/our knowledge.

Seller Signature: _____

Date: _____

Instructions for Use:
- **Complete Each Section**: For each item, select "Yes" or "No" and provide additional details where necessary.
- **Seek Legal Guidance**: Consult with a real estate attorney to ensure this form meets state requirements and includes all legally required disclosures.
- **Provide to Buyer**: Give a completed, signed copy of this form to any prospective buyers, ensuring full disclosure as part of the sales process.

Appendix E: Buyer Inquiry and Follow-Up Log

Buyer Name	Contact Information	Preferred Contact Method	Date of Initial Inquiry	Inquiry Details	Follow-Up Date	Notes on Follow-Up & Buyer Feedback	Next Steps / Actions

Instructions for Use:

- **Log Each Inquiry**: For every buyer who inquires, record their contact details, preferred method of communication, and date of inquiry.
- **Follow-Up**: Document each follow-up date and add notes based on buyer feedback or specific points discussed.
- **Plan Next Steps**: Use the "Next Steps / Actions" column to plan further actions, like scheduling a showing, sending more property information, or following up on interest level.

Appendix F: Offer Comparison Worksheet

Offer Detail	Offer 1	Offer 2	Offer 3
Offer Amount			
Proposed Closing Date			
Contingencies (e.g., inspection, financing)			
Financing Type (Cash, Mortgage)			
Mortgage Approval Status			
Earnest Money Deposit			
Additional Terms/Concessions			
Estimated Closing Costs			
Repair Requests			
Other Notable Factors			

Instructions for Use:

- **Record Offer Details**: For each offer, document the offer amount, proposed closing date, financing details, and any contingencies (e.g., inspection or financing).
- **Compare Terms and Costs**: Note additional terms, concessions, and repair requests for each offer. Include estimated closing costs or any other associated expenses.
- **Evaluate**: Use this side-by-side comparison to evaluate the strengths and weaknesses of each offer, making it easier to choose the most favorable deal.

Appendix G: FSBO Sales Contract Template

Property Address: _____

Buyer(s): _____

Seller(s): _____

Date of Agreement: _____

1. Purchase Price and Payment Terms

- **Purchase Price:** $_____
- **Earnest Money Deposit:** $_____, to be paid by Buyer upon acceptance of this contract.
- **Payment Terms:**
  - Cash
  - Financing/Mortgage
  - Other: _____

2. Closing Date and Possession

  - **Closing Date:** _____
  - **Possession Date:** _____ (Date when Buyer will take possession)

3. Property Description and Included Items

- **Legal Description of Property**: _____

  _____

- **Fixtures and Items Included in Sale**:
  - Appliances: Refrigerator, oven, dishwasher, etc.
  - Other: Light fixtures, window treatments, ceiling fans, etc.
- **Excluded Items** (if any): _____

  _____

4. Contingencies

- **Financing Contingency**: Buyer's obligation to close is contingent on obtaining financing approval.
- **Inspection Contingency**: Buyer has the right to inspect the property within ____ days.
- **Appraisal Contingency**: The sale is contingent on property appraising at or above the purchase price.
- **Other Contingencies**: _____

  _____

5. Disclosures

- **Seller Disclosures**: Seller agrees to provide a full disclosure of known issues, including but not limited to:
  - Lead-based paint (if applicable)
  - Structural or foundational issues
  - Plumbing, electrical, or HVAC problems
- **Inspection Period**: Buyer has ____ days to conduct inspections and notify Seller of any issues.

6. Legal Obligations and Closing Costs

- **Closing Costs**:
  - Seller's Responsibility: Title search, property taxes, deed preparation, etc.

- o Buyer's Responsibility: Mortgage fees, inspection fees, recording fees, etc.
- **Prorations**: Property taxes and HOA fees (if applicable) will be prorated as of the closing date.
- **Other Obligations**: _____ _____

7. Default and Remedies

- If Buyer defaults, Seller may retain the earnest money deposit as liquidated damages.
- If Seller defaults, Buyer may pursue specific performance or the return of the earnest money.

8. Additional Terms and Conditions

- _____
- _____

9. Signatures

- **Seller Signature**: _____
- **Date**: _____
- **Buyer Signature**: _____
- **Date**: _____

Instructions for Use:

- **Complete Each Section**: Fill in specific details regarding purchase price, contingencies, payment terms, and closing costs.
- **Attach Property Disclosures**: Include a copy of the completed Property Disclosure Form as part of this contract.
- **Seek Legal Review**: A real estate attorney should review this form to ensure compliance with state laws and address any unique terms or conditions.

Appendix H: Closing Checklist

Property Address: _____

Seller(s): _____

Buyer(s):_____

Scheduled Closing Date: _____

Closing Task	Date Completed	Notes
1. Financing and Appraisal Confirmation		Confirm buyer's loan approval and appraisal
2. Home Inspection Completion		Ensure inspection has been completed
3. Negotiate/Complete Any Necessary Repairs		Address repair requests if applicable
4. Verify Property Title Search and Insurance		Confirm clear title and insurance coverage
5. Transfer Utilities		Schedule transfer for gas, electricity, water, etc.
6. Schedule Final Walk-Through		Confirm with buyer 24-48 hours before closing
7. Review Closing Documents		Review deed, settlement statement, etc.
8. Prepare and Transfer Keys/Access Codes		Hand over all keys, codes, garage openers
9. Notify Homeowners Association (if applicable)		Notify HOA of ownership transfer

10. Final Prorations and Adjustments		Finalize property tax, HOA, and utility prorations
11. Obtain Closing Funds		Confirm payment method and prepare funds
12. Sign All Required Documents		Both parties sign final closing documents

Instructions for Use:

1. **Complete Each Task**: Mark each task's completion date and add notes if needed, detailing any arrangements or specific instructions.
2. **Coordinate with Buyer**: Ensure that the buyer is aware of all necessary steps, such as the final walk-through and utility transfers.
3. **Review with Closing Agent or Attorney**: Work with your closing agent or at

Appendix I: Post-Sale Expense and Profit Calculation Sheet

Property Address: _____

Sale Date: _____

1. Sales Details

Description	Amount ($)
Total Sale Price	
Earnest Money Deposit Received	
Commission Savings (5-6%)	

2. FSBO-Related Expenses

Expense Category	Amount ($)
Flat-Fee MLS Listing	
Professional Photography	
Videography/Virtual Tour	
Staging	
Targeted Advertising	
Legal Consultation	
Pre-Listing Appraisal	
Pre-Listing Inspection	
Miscellaneous Fees (e.g., signs)	
Total FSBO Expenses	

3. Additional Closing Costs

Description	Amount ($)
Title Insurance	
Closing Agent/Attorney Fees	
Prorated Property Taxes	
Homeowners Association Fees	
Other Closing Costs	
Total Additional Closing Costs	

4. Estimated Taxes and Deductions

Description	Amount ($)
Capital Gains Tax (if applicable)	
State/Local Tax Fees	
Other Tax Implications	
Total Taxes and Deductions	

5. Final Profit Calculation

Calculation	Amount ($)
Total Sale Price	
Minus Total FSBO Expenses	
Minus Total Additional Closing Costs	
Minus Total Taxes and Deductions	
Net Profit	

Instructions for Use:

1. **Fill in Each Section**: Start with the total sale price, then itemize all FSBO-related expenses, closing costs, and taxes or fees.
2. **Calculate Final Profit**: Subtract total expenses, closing costs, and tax deductions from the sale price to determine net profit.
3. **Review with Financial Advisor** (if applicable): Consult a financial advisor for guidance on taxes and other deductions, especially for high-value sales.

Appendix J: iComparative Market Analysis (CMA) Worksheet

Purpose: Helps FSBO sellers conduct a detailed analysis of comparable properties to set an accurate, competitive listing price.

Comparable Property Address	Square Footage (sq ft)	Lot Size (acres)	Bedrooms	Bathrooms	Other Features	Sale Price ($)	Closing Date	Price per Square Foot ($)
1.								
2.								
3.								
4.								
5.								
6.								
7.								
8.								
9.								
10.								

Usage: Fill in each row with details of comparable properties in your area. This worksheet will help you assess the market value of your property based on recently sold homes nearby, providing a realistic starting point for pricing.

Appendix K: Pricing Adjustment Log

Purpose: Tracks all pricing adjustments made during the listing period and provides reasoning for each, allowing FSBO sellers to monitor the impact of adjustments.

Date of Adjust-ment	New Listing Price ($)	Reason for Adjustment	Buyer Interest Post-Ad-justment (Inquiries/ Offers)	Notes
1.				
2.				
3.				
4.				
5.				
6.				
7.				
8.				
9.				
10.				

Usage: Each time a price adjustment is made, record the new listing price, the reason behind the change, and any changes in buyer interest afterward. This log will help you assess the effectiveness of each adjustment and guide future pricing decisions.

Here's a printable version of the **Buyer Interest and Feedback Log** for easy tracking of buyer interactions and feedback on the property.

Appendix L: Buyer Interest and Feedback Log

Purpose: Helps sellers track inquiries, showings, and buyer feedback to assess the market's response to the property's price.

Date of Inquiry/ Showing	Buyer Feed-back on Price	Level of Interest (Low/Medium/High)	Fol-low-Up Actions	Notes
1.				
2.				
3.				
4.				
5.				
6.				
7.				
8.				
9.				
10.				

Usage: Use this log to document each interaction with potential buyers, their feedback on pricing or property condition, and their level of interest. Review this information periodically to make informed adjustments to your listing and stay competitive.

Appendix M: Pre-Listing Price Decision Summary

Purpose: Summarizes the final listing price decision and rationale, ensuring FSBO sellers have a clear, objective foundation for their initial price.

Section	Details
Chosen Listing Price	
Market Data Summary	Key insights from Comparative Market Analysis (CMA), historical pricing trends, and competitive analysis.
Pricing Model Chosen	Specify the model used: Market-based pricing, anchor pricing, psychological pricing, etc.
Adjustment Plan	Timeframe for price reviews and adjustments (e.g., every 30 days based on buyer feedback and market data).
Rationale	Unique property features, recent upgrades, or other factors that influenced the initial price decision.

Usage: This summary provides a baseline for the initial pricing strategy, helping sellers maintain consistency and objectivity in setting their listing price and ensuring they have a structured approach for future adjustments if needed.

Appendix N: Post-Sale Considerations Checklist

Purpose: Assists FSBO sellers in completing all necessary steps after the sale, including the move-out process, tax preparation, and key handover.

Section	Tasks	Completed
1. Moving Out and Handover of Keys		
Move-Out Timeline	Establish and confirm timeline based on closing date	

Hiring Movers	Schedule movers or arrange for rental truck, if needed	
Packing and Decluttering	Organize and begin packing, discard unneeded items	
Cleaning and Repairs	Clean property thoroughly, perform any minor repairs agreed upon in the sale	
Utility Disconnection	Schedule utility disconnection (electricity, gas, water) for the closing date	
Mail Forwarding	Set up mail forwarding to new address	
2. Key Handover and Property Access		
Prepare Key Copies	Ensure all required keys are prepared for the buyer (doors, garage, storage)	
Document Condition	Take photos or video of property's condition on handover day	
Transfer Property Documents	Provide necessary property documents (warranties, manuals, etc.)	
Final Walk-Through with Buyer	Coordinate a final walk-through if possible	
3. Tax Implications and Capital Gains		
Determine Capital Gains	Calculate profit from sale and determine if it exceeds exemption limits	

Primary Residence Exemption	Confirm eligibility for primary residence exemption (2 of last 5 years as primary residence)	
Identify Short or Long-Term Gains	Check holding period to determine if sale qualifies for long-term or short-term capital gains	
4. Deductions and Adjustments to Capital Gains		
Track Improvements and Selling Costs	Gather receipts for home improvements, renovations, and selling costs	
Depreciation Recapture Check	Review potential depreciation recapture if property was previously rented	
State and Local Tax Implications	Consult state/local tax requirements for real estate sale tax	
5. Documentation for Tax Purposes		
Maintain Records	Keep copies of sale agreement, closing statement, and all related documents	
Consult Tax Professional	Meet with a tax advisor for guidance on exemptions and accurate reporting	

Usage: Sellers should complete each section of this checklist to ensure a seamless move-out, property handover, and compliance with tax requirements.

CHAPTER 8
BONUS RESOURCES

FSBO Checklist

A step-by-step checklist to guide FSBO sellers through each stage of the selling process, from listing preparation to post-sale considerations. Go to www.DIYFlexRealty.com for Sample Contracts by signing up and enjoy the many resources available for your continued success!

1. Sample Contracts And Templates

- **Purchase and Sale Agreement**
  - This contract details the terms and conditions of the sale between buyer and seller, including price, contingencies, and closing date.
- **Property Disclosure Form**
  - Used to disclose known property defects, environmental hazards, and repairs, ensuring transparency and compliance with legal requirements.
- **Lead-Based Paint Disclosure (for homes built before 1978)**
  - Required by federal law to inform buyers about potential lead hazards in older homes.
- **Bill of Sale**
  - Provides a detailed list of any personal property included in the sale, such as appliances or furniture.
- **Addendum for Inspection Contingency**

- o Specifies the terms for property inspection, including timelines and potential adjustments based on inspection results.
- **Financing Addendum**
  - o Details conditions related to buyer financing, such as loan approval and down payment, providing contingencies if financing falls through.
- **Counteroffer Form**
  - o A document used to outline any changes to the terms of an initial offer from a buyer, such as price adjustments or additional contingencies.
- **Earnest Money Agreement**
  - o Details the terms related to the earnest money deposit, including amount, holding location, and conditions for refund or forfeiture.
- **Closing Statement**
  - o A breakdown of financial transactions involved in the sale, including proceeds to the seller, costs paid by the buyer, and other closing fees.

2. Recommended Tools And Services

1. **Property Valuation Tools**
   - o Zillow Zestimate, Redfin Estimate, and Realtor.com to gauge property value.
2. **Flat-Fee MLS Services**
   - o Providers like Houzeo or FSBO.com offer MLS listing packages that maximize visibility without full agent representation.
3. **Professional Photography Services**

    ○ High-quality photography improves listing appeal; platforms like Thumbtack or local photography directories can connect sellers with professionals.

4. **Real Estate Attorney Services**

    ○ For contract review and compliance, FSBO sellers can use legal service marketplaces like Avvo or find a real estate attorney through their state bar association.

Appendix M: State-by-State Real Estate Resources Index

A comprehensive index with hyperlinks to each U.S. state's official real estate commission or regulatory agency. This index will allow FSBO sellers to access their specific state's guidelines, forms, and requirements for FSBO transactions and property sales regulations.

U.S. State Real Estate Resources Index

State	Real Estate Regulatory Agency/ Commission	Website Link
Alabama	Alabama Real Estate Commission	arec.alabama.gov
Alaska	Alaska Real Estate Commission	commerce.alaska.gov/web/cbpl
Arizona	Arizona Department of Real Estate	azre.gov
Arkansas	Arkansas Real Estate Commission	arec.arkansas.gov
California	California Department of Real Estate	dre.ca.gov
Colorado	Colorado Division of Real Estate	dora.colorado.gov/dre
Connecticut	Connecticut Real Estate Commission	portal.ct.gov/dcp

Delaware	Delaware Real Estate Commission	dpr.delaware.gov
Florida	Florida Real Estate Commission (FREC)	myfloridalicense.com
Georgia	Georgia Real Estate Commission & Appraisers Board	grec.state.ga.us
Hawaii	Hawaii Real Estate Branch, Department of Commerce and Consumer Affairs	cca.hawaii.gov/reb
Idaho	Idaho Real Estate Commission	irec.idaho.gov
Illinois	Illinois Department of Financial & Professional Regulation - Division of Real Estate	idfpr.com
Indiana	Indiana Real Estate Commission	in.gov/pla/real.htm
Iowa	Iowa Real Estate Commission	plb.iowa.gov
Kansas	Kansas Real Estate Commission	krec.ks.gov
Kentucky	Kentucky Real Estate Commission	krec.ky.gov
Louisiana	Louisiana Real Estate Commission	lrec.gov
Maine	Maine Real Estate Commission	maine.gov/pfr/ professionallicensing
Maryland	Maryland Real Estate Commission	dllr.state.md.us

Massachusetts	Massachusetts Board of Registration of Real Estate Brokers and Salespersons	mass.gov/dpl
Michigan	Michigan Department of Licensing and Regulatory Affairs (LARA)	michigan.gov/lara
Minnesota	Minnesota Department of Commerce - Real Estate Licensing	mn.gov/commerce
Mississippi	Mississippi Real Estate Commission	mrec.ms.gov
Missouri	Missouri Real Estate Commission	pr.mo.gov/realestate
Montana	Montana Board of Realty Regulation	boards.bsd.dli.mt.gov
Nebraska	Nebraska Real Estate Commission	nrec.nebraska.gov
Nevada	Nevada Real Estate Division	red.nv.gov
New Hampshire	New Hampshire Real Estate Commission	oplc.nh.gov/real-estate
New Jersey	New Jersey Real Estate Commission	state.nj.us/dobi/division_rec.htm
New Mexico	New Mexico Real Estate Commission	rld.state.nm.us
New York	New York State Division of Licensing Services	dos.ny.gov
North Carolina	North Carolina Real Estate Commission	ncrec.gov

North Dakota	North Dakota Real Estate Commission	realestatend.org
Ohio	Ohio Division of Real Estate & Professional Licensing	com.ohio.gov/real
Oklahoma	Oklahoma Real Estate Commission	orec.ok.gov
Oregon	Oregon Real Estate Agency	oregon.gov/rea
Pennsylvania	Pennsylvania Real Estate Commission	dos.pa.gov
Rhode Island	Rhode Island Department of Business Regulation - Real Estate	dbr.ri.gov
South Carolina	South Carolina Real Estate Commission	llr.sc.gov/rec
South Dakota	South Dakota Real Estate Commission	dlr.sd.gov/realestate
Tennessee	Tennessee Real Estate Commission	tn.gov/commerce
Texas	Texas Real Estate Commission (TREC)	trec.texas.gov
Utah	Utah Division of Real Estate	realestate.utah.gov
Vermont	Vermont Real Estate Commission	sos.vermont.gov
Virginia	Virginia Department of Professional and Occupational Regulation - Real Estate Board	dpor.virginia.gov

Washington	Washington State Department of Licensing - Real Estate Licensing	dol.wa.gov
West Virginia	West Virginia Real Estate Commission	rec.wv.gov
Wisconsin	Wisconsin Department of Safety and Professional Services - Real Estate	dsps.wi.gov
Wyoming	Wyoming Real Estate Commission	realestate.wyo.gov

This index provides a centralized resource for FSBO sellers to access guidelines, forms, and specific requirements for each state's real estate regulatory agency. You can hyperlink the URLs directly within your document for quick access.

3. Fsbo Checklist

1. Pre-Listing Preparation

- Research Your Market: Study local real estate trends, recent comparable sales (comps), and the pricing strategies of similar homes in your area.
- Set a Competitive Price: Use tools like Zillow's Zestimate, Redfin's Estimate, or a Comparative Market Analysis (CMA) to set a realistic, market-aligned price.
- Complete Any Necessary Repairs: Inspect the property and make repairs to increase appeal; consider minor renovations or updates that add value.
- Declutter and Depersonalize: Remove personal items and reduce clutter to make the home more appealing and spacious for potential buyers.

- Stage Your Home: Stage rooms to highlight the property's best features. Arrange furniture and décor to make rooms feel larger and more inviting.
- Hire a Professional Photographer: Quality photos can significantly improve online listing appeal, so consider professional photography.
- Gather Property Documents: Collect necessary documents such as the property deed, recent utility bills, property tax statements, warranties, and manuals for appliances.

2. Create a Compelling Listing

- Craft an Effective Listing Description: Write a detailed, engaging description highlighting key features (e.g., recent upgrades, unique aspects, and neighborhood amenities).
- List on FSBO Websites: Post on FSBO platforms such as Zillow, Realtor.com, and Redfin.
- Consider a Flat-Fee MLS Service: Gain MLS exposure by listing through a flat-fee MLS service to reach a broader audience.
- Promote on Social Media: Use Facebook, Instagram, and other social platforms to share your listing with a wider audience.
- Create Virtual Tours or Videos: Video walkthroughs can attract out-of-town buyers and provide additional transparency.

3. Implement Marketing Strategies

- Set Up a Yard Sign: Place an FSBO sign in front of your property to attract local attention.
- Create Flyers or Brochures: Print high-quality flyers with property details and distribute them in the neighborhood, local community boards, and nearby coffee shops.
- Advertise in Local Listings: Consider posting in neighborhood newsletters, local online classifieds, or community bulletin boards.

- Host Open Houses: Plan an open house and promote it through your listing and social media. Prepare sign-in sheets to gather contact information from attendees.

4. Manage Inquiries and Showings

- Pre-Screen Potential Buyers: Pre-qualify buyers by asking about financing and their buying timeline. Request a mortgage pre-approval letter to ensure seriousness.
- Schedule Showings: Set up a system for scheduling showings and prepare the home for each visit.
- Provide Property Disclosures: Prepare and provide a disclosure statement that outlines any known defects or issues with the property.
- Keep Track of Buyer Feedback: After showings, record feedback from potential buyers to identify areas of improvement or to adjust pricing if necessary.

5. Negotiate Offers

- Review All Offers Carefully: Assess each offer based on price, contingencies, financing type, and proposed closing date.
- Make Counteroffers if Needed: Don't hesitate to negotiate on price or terms if the initial offer doesn't meet your expectations.
- Request Earnest Money Deposits: Ensure that serious buyers include earnest money with their offer to demonstrate commitment.
- Consider Contingencies: Review contingencies (e.g., financing, inspection) and consider how they may impact the sale.
- Document All Negotiations: Keep a record of offers, counteroffers, and responses for legal clarity and future reference.

6. Finalize the Contract and Prepare for Closing

- Complete a Purchase Agreement: Use a standardized FSBO purchase agreement or have a real estate attorney draft the contract to outline terms and obligations.
- Hire a Real Estate Attorney: Many states recommend or require a real estate attorney to review the contract, especially for FSBO transactions.
- Schedule a Home Inspection: If the buyer requests a home inspection, arrange for it to occur within the agreed-upon timeframe.
- Resolve Any Inspection Contingencies: If issues are uncovered during the inspection, negotiate repairs or credits with the buyer.
- Order an Appraisal if Required: If the buyer is financing, their lender will likely require an appraisal to determine the property's value.

7. Prepare for Closing

- Coordinate with a Title Company or Escrow Agent: Arrange for title insurance, which protects both you and the buyer from potential title issues.
- Obtain a Closing Statement: The title company or attorney will provide a closing statement detailing all financial aspects of the transaction, including taxes, fees, and the remaining mortgage balance.
- Schedule Utility Transfers: Arrange for final utility readings and transfer utilities to the buyer's name on the closing day.
- Clear the Property and Move Out: Ensure all personal items are removed, and the home is cleaned before the handover.
- Prepare for the Final Walk-Through: The buyer may wish to conduct a final walk-through to verify that the property is in agreed-upon condition.

8. Closing Day

- Sign All Required Documents: During the closing meeting, both you and the buyer will sign necessary documents, including the deed transfer and any mortgage payoff statements.
- Transfer Keys and Access Codes: Hand over all keys, garage door openers, and any access codes to the buyer at closing.
- Receive Payment: After all documents are signed and funds are transferred, you will receive the payment for your property, either by check or wire transfer.
- Store Final Documents: Keep copies of the closing documents, including the final settlement statement and transfer documents, for tax purposes and future reference.

9. Post-Sale Considerations

- Settle Any Outstanding Bills: Pay off remaining balances for property taxes, HOA fees, or any pending utilities.
- Review Capital Gains Tax Implications: Consult with a tax professional to understand potential tax obligations on your capital gains.
- Forward Mail and Update Your Address: Set up mail forwarding with USPS and update your address with relevant institutions.
- Document Capital Improvements: Retain records of capital improvements made to the property as they may impact your tax basis in future transactions.

Recommended Tools and Services

- Property Valuation Tools: Zillow Zestimate, Redfin Estimate, Realtor.com
- Professional Photography: Thumbtack, local photography directories
- MLS Services: www.DIYFlexRealty.com, FSBO.com, Houzeo

- Real Estate Attorney Services: Avvo, local bar associations

This FSBO checklist was created to ensure sellers have access to navigate each step of the home-selling process efficiently, covering all bases from pre-listing preparation to post-sale follow-ups. By following each step, sellers can maintain organization, compliance, and focus, resulting in a smoother FSBO transaction.

AFTERWORD

Thank you for taking the journey through this comprehensive guide to For Sale By Owner (FSBO) home selling. By exploring each step, from initial preparation to closing and post-sale considerations, you've gained insights, tools, and strategies that empower you to handle the FSBO process with confidence. This guide is meant not just as a roadmap but as a companion to help you overcome challenges, make informed decisions, and ultimately achieve the rewarding outcome of selling your property on your own terms.

FSBO can seem daunting, but it also brings immense satisfaction and autonomy. You've navigated the complexities of real estate transactions, equipped with a clear understanding of market dynamics, pricing strategies, legal requirements, and marketing tactics. Embracing the FSBO process allows you to connect with buyers directly, build lasting relationships, and leave a meaningful impression on those who will make your property their own.

DIY Flex Realty is proud to be a part of this journey, supporting independent sellers like you in every aspect of your sale. Remember, whether it's your first time selling FSBO or one of many, each experience brings new learning and growth. We're grateful to have provided you with tools and insights, and we look forward to supporting you in future endeavors.

I wish you continued success!

www.ingramcontent.com/pod-product-compliance
Lightning Source LLC
Chambersburg PA
CBHW071702210326
41597CB00017B/2288